Is There Any Ice Cream?

Judith Allen Shone

 FriesenPress

Suite 300 - 990 Fort St
Victoria, BC, V8V 3K2
Canada

www.friesenpress.com

Copyright © 2019 by Judith Allen Shone
First Edition — 2019

Cover design and caregiver card design by Judith Allen Shone.

Original lilac and flower illustrations by artist, ©Mitrushova, Mitrushova Art. Used with her permission, with licenses from fotolia.com. Original Wafer cone photograph by artist, © Jiri Hera, with license from dreamstime.com.

DISCLAIMER: These stories are for entertainment only and are not intended as a caregiver guide. Author has no medical training. There is absolutely no intention to advise or suggest diagnosis or treatment, of any kind, related to any illness, in any situation. Suggestion would be for readers to consult a health care provider for guidance as appropriate.

ISBN
978-1-5255-5123-9 (Hardcover)
978-1-5255-5124-6 (Paperback)
978-1-5255-5125-3 (eBook)

1. BIOGRAPHY & AUTOBIOGRAPHY, PERSONAL MEMOIRS

Distributed to the trade by The Ingram Book Company

CONTENTS

Is There Any Ice Cream?

Surviving the Challenges of Caregiving for a Loved One with Dementia, Anxiety, and COPD

Accepting the Gift of Caregiving, Part One

By Judith Allen Shone

 DEDICATION

To My Love, my partner and companion. Together, we did the best we could.

To our phenomenal Lifeliner Group, whom we met on Wednesday morning for coffee for years.

# START THE CONVERSATION

"What is it like to be a caregiver?" I have been asked this many times.

It is difficult to describe, especially to those who have never been one. I am talking about caregiving for someone with dementia, but I suspect being a caregiver for someone with any disease might be just as overwhelming.

In the beginning, the concept of caregiving was beyond my horizon. And I realized it was also beyond the scope of many who had not been in the company of another caregiver or one with memory loss.

When a group of caregivers agreed that we all wished we had had helpful ways to explain our situations, I was prompted to create this "I need you to know" graphic description.

For most caregivers I knew, the words "desperate and overwhelming" described it. But for others, this graphic depiction showed what caregiving felt like. It seemed like a more precise message.

This visual has helped bring understanding into the conversations of families and friends where at first it was difficult to bring up the topic or to discuss memory loss at all.

Share this caregiver graphic to help start your conversation. Download 4" x 6" in color from _www. caregiveralzheimerstory.com/caregiver-feels_. Place it where others will see it. Allow it to stimulate a conversation that could help you explain your life as it really is. Maybe it will encourage questions.

I hope this image and this book will generate understanding of the caregiving world and help bring meaningful support into each caregiver's life.

 AUTHOR'S NOTE

Although these stories are about My Love and me, I have tried to be sensitive to the situations of the people around us and thus have used very few names. I hoped to prevent unintended consequences while preserving and passing on the heart and soul of each experience, not to immortalize, but to share. While, in some cases, there had to be slight alteration to condense seven years into a five-page chapter, for the most part, these stories are based on true events, as best I could recall them. Forgive me if my memory didn't get it perfectly right. Conversations are not from a transcript, but from my notes and recall of the core of issues. I smoothed out the confusing time-lines we lived.

One friend asked if I had written a love story. I did not think so at the outset, but as I re-read my journey journal chapters, they revealed an answer. I found a story of love. A love for My Love, for those who surrounded us, and a love for humanity. It is hard to think of this story without being filled with the love shared with me and My Love by so many people.

As I wrote, I recognized that, over time, I was learning to be more sensitive, more empathetic, and hopefully more compassionate. I am working on patience. Learning to cope with the wide-ranging responsibility of the life of another solely in my hands took meditation, reflection, and gut-wrenching cries to accept.

A thin thread through the story reveals my resistance, but in the end, I had no choice. He needed me, as his caregiver, to be there for him as his ally and advocate. To get to each of the heartbreaking moments of decision, I had to work through unbelievable sorrow, despair, and hopelessness to get to acceptance, most times alone.

I am glad I finally made the decision to accept the gift of caregiving. I'd like to believe I became a better person as my experience unexpectedly revealed a beautiful enrichment to my life.

Many times, hearing shared experiences can reduce fears, transform denial, ease loneliness, and even change perspectives and expectations. While there are many caregiver stories, I believe these stories can generate an appreciation for caregivers and of caregiving. I hope my words will encourage reaching out to find those who are reaching back. Caregivers need the self-care and friendships that support provides.

I was troubled that many of these events could have happened at all, yet they did. As you read, you, too, may feel exhausted!

Welcome to my world,
Judith Allen Shone
2019

 APPRECIATION

In truth, some of the people who helped me give birth to the *Accepting the Gift of Caregiving* stories are from my youth. I am grateful their paths crossed mine. Unknowingly, they planted seeds. I harvested what felt right and kept propagating. Adding reassurance and inspiration to the collection of growing, positive intentions enabled me to show up in the garden of possibilities.

Because I would feel horrible forgetting someone, I am not using names. I must emphasize that so many who touched our lives had an impact, from the staff at the pharmacy, to the hospital volunteers, to one amazing personal service worker.

Specifically, I thank Musician Clinic physicians, therapists who first listened to me talk in stories and then encouraged me to put the words on paper, helping me realize I had my perspective to share with other caregivers. My fears lessened when I heard, "You take care of him. We'll take care of you." I feel so much appreciation.

It had to be serendipity that I had counselors and therapists who listened and whose wisdom guided me. I appreciated the calls to be sure I was ok. They understood. Thank you.

Hugs to my siblings and my children who read the pages and encouraged me to "keep going," particularly my daughter, who, with my grand-daughter, offered to put eyes on the manuscript to help proof and edit.

Although I had never been an enthusiastic groupie, our Lifeliner Group, made up of caregivers and their loved ones, gave me strength and support, conversation, hugs, purple birds, holiday and birth-day dinners, strawberry cakes, shortcake, home-made fruitcake, and Argentine Malbec wine. How can one ever reciprocate for such care and generos-ity? Grateful.

Those same friends insisted my stories, and others like them, needed to be told and to be heard. They encouraged me to express experiences as true-to-life as I could. We knew, because we'd met them, that many caregivers were suffering in silence or were overwhelmed from lack of practical and meaningful connections. We wanted to encourage those caregivers.

The Group cheered me on, knowing what I was sharing was somewhat similar to what they, too, were living. We also hoped that through these words, many associates with health organizations and possibly even government health workers and officials might feel the emotional chaos we lived . . . maybe feeling our personal milestones of endurance could help them help us. Thank you, Lifeliners.

By the time I reached my seventy-fifth birthday, I knew I did not get there on my own! I recognized that I needed other people in my life. These stories were no different. It "took a village" for these pages to materialize.

The universe showered our village with stellar, compassionate medical professionals and health practitioners. I learned how much they truly cared. We especially thank My Love's persistent personal physician, plus his geriatrician and nurse practitioner, and their associates and referrals, all of whom kept looking under every rock for answers. The office nurses and staff were equally as caring and attentive, as were their clinic of associates, who each had a part in searching for My Love's various diagnoses along the way. The hospital staff and technicians during My Love's visits could not have been more helpful. There was no end to how our village was blessed. Indebted.

Everyone we interacted with in our local Alzheimer Society of Hamilton Halton, and the many volunteers who returned year after year, seemed to have their special treasure chest of HOPE to share art, exercise, friendship, professional counseling, support cafés, education, strategies, and therapies. And the best part was that it seemed all just for My Love and for me. We were so fortunate to have their knowledge to draw from week in, week out. I could not have endured our journey without their guidance. So much gratitude.

We were privileged to have Acclaim Health in our region who were ready with personal support, service workers, guidance, and kindness. Thank you to the host of care angels, attentive senior daycare staff, and provincial health care coordinators. These folks were so vital, providing support and information regarding issues that were of paramount importance to caregivers and to me.

I am indebted to those who supported me, those who unknowingly encouraged me in my role as solo caregiver and supported my need for periodic relief from my daily tasks or moments of desperation. Thank you to my secret angel who gifted me with therapeutic touch; you knew caregivers needed love too. *Merci beaucoup.*

How fortunate we were to live in an apartment building where the superintendent, manager, and staff had experienced life with one with dementia. They understood. Bless them.

To strangers who became friends who shared love and understanding, thank you for reaching out with gifts of wisdom and support at just the right times. A warm smile from each stranger generated one in me. My heart smiled back.

To those in town, across the continent, across the ocean, and online, I thank you for connecting with me and to our village, a confirmation that space and time cannot interrupt enduring friendships.

I hold dear that every single one of us was able to spend time together in our village. Your expressions of love lifted me up to carry on. I am humbled by the world of love where we live.

Grateful acknowledgement is made for permissions from authors to publish their words.

Journey Note:

"I began to realize that I could not make sense of his world, and that My Love could not teach me."

—Judith Allen Shone, author, *Is There Any Ice Cream?: Surviving the Challenges of Caregiving for a Loved One with Dementia, Anxiety, and COPD*

INTRODUCTION –
IMMERSED IN DESPAIR

If only we could turn back time!

The Alzheimer Society called it "ambiguous loss" when one lost a loved one progressively, memory by memory. When I found it online and read the Society's brochure *Ambiguous Loss and Grief in Dementia: A resource for individuals and families,* I only began to understand my mixed feelings and sense of ambiguity, which for me redefined loss and grief.

It was painful to read "closure is not possible, and your grief cannot be fully resolved, while the person with dementia" lives. I had trouble comprehending that once the memories vanished, they were gone. It was even harder to realize that one day I, too, would become a lost memory.

My Love and I sat in his hospital room last spring celebrating our twenty-fourth anniversary playing Go-Fish. Each other's third partner and in our seventies, we had been growing old gracefully together. And then our life had been turned topsy-turvy by COPD, Alzheimer's disease, and anxiety attacks, and especially by elevated calcium. Instead of living out my retirement dreams, I was trying to learn strategies for reducing stress. Instead of reading travel brochures, I was learning about long-term care.

Because we met in our fifties, I didn't know My Love in his active, younger years. I heard from his twin brother and his daughters that he loved skiing, swimming, and boating. In his middle years, he had spent many hours both working and operating his exhibit business. Did I mention boating?

Three years before I went to work for his company, My Love and I met at a trade show, where I unsuccessfully gave my best efforts to capture his client's business. As anyone might imagine, My Love never spoke to me again, well, not until he interviewed me and borrowed my glasses to read my resume.

That's a strange introductory approach, I thought.

For the next three years, our paths crossed in company meetings.

Then, during a flight to a week-long trade show, we got to talking. Our unintended relationship should never have happened. As with affairs, it was not "right." But it happened. And then, one day, he showed up at my apartment door with three bulging green garbage bags. He was moving in. Regrettably, there were heartaches to go around.

Love ignores things it shouldn't sometimes. And so, our relationship was a whim that turned into a very long affair of over twenty-five years. Married or not, my heartbeats, my thoughts, my narratives mirrored my honest caring for another human being.

The thing was, we enjoyed being together. My Love was a gentle person; I never thought of him as abusive. I always thought it was our creative spirits that connected. In life, people do change; people do find new partners. We did.

By the time of My Love's diagnosis, we had been together for twenty years. During those years, we shared our passion for art; we traveled a bit; and we boated on the lake and in the Caribbean. Together we attended trade shows across North America. We had planned to do an ocean-to-gulf-to-ocean drive in our retirement. But nothing prepared us for the journey that unfolded after My Love developed illnesses that challenged many medical professionals.

It had never occurred to me to ask, "What if he gets very sick and I, alone, have to be the one to take care of him for a long time?" But that is exactly what happened. This is that story. I carried on as if the next day were the same as the one before. I didn't feel the subtle shifts in our life until we were deep into our new routines.

No one warned me we would go through periods of hell. I never expected to experience the emotions that dragged me to near-depression. I had no idea how terrified I had become until I recognized I was looking out from inside my bubble again.

Thankfully, I was able to convert thoughts into words, making my mental experience seem less harsh. That adaptation was something I must have done instinctively for my sanity.

For the most part, I wrote about our journey from the "better" sides. I never wanted to experience the extreme negatives twice, so I let them float away, never to reach these pages, hopefully forgotten. It was far too overwhelming to revisit situations I had already worked through and left behind.

Eventually, the chosen stories evolved into a suite I named *Accepting the Gift of Caregiving*.

Is There Any Ice Cream? reflects on those unexpected moments and unintended experiences when I desperately resisted becoming My Love's caregiver, just three years into our retirement. The ensuing emotions, developing illnesses, and the caregiving journey are woven together, revealing one story that touches on the phases of My Love's unfolding fatal diseases.

Before you read, consider:

1. My motto: As a caregiver, each day, do something that makes *your* heart sing.

2. My caution: If you notice an increase in your personal stressors or are experiencing an abnormal period of turmoil in your life (some call it compassion fatigue, others might refer to it as caregiver burnout) then, please, care for your own signs and symptoms before you do another thing. Caregivers need care too. You could choose to read this book in small snippets, waiting until you feel comfortable reading about or discussing caregiver activities. I do not want you to increase your anguish.

3. My message: Find the Alzheimer Society, or a similar organization, nearest you and call them. If possible, do not wait. Get help any time you experience something you don't understand, for you as well as for your loved one. Lifelines are essential. Join support groups and be socially active with other caregivers. Take that one, break-the-ice, first step. Remember, it is important to know who to call on your journey. Supportive and understanding friends will make your burden lighter.

4. My wish: Although at first I did not, I now believe we all possess an inner capacity for caregiving. While we may not envision that for ourselves, as I did not, my wish for all caregivers and those who support them is that they are able to accept their role as a treasure we have been given, a gift of experience.

Ultimately, I see caregiving as a gift we give to each other while on this planet.

You might be a caregiver, or perhaps you will become one. Maybe you support a caregiver, or possibly will need one to care for you. I have found so many beautiful role model caregivers. You will too.

Normally, I was the only witness to My Love's behaviors. I wished others had been with me to attest to what I was observing—other caregivers, other family members, other friends, even those in the medical field. But they were seldom nearby. I was the only one.

As a caregiver, sometimes my future seemed to be characterized by long, lonely days, forecasting a grim outlook that might go on for years. How could I anticipate despair?

Knowing other caregivers might be on the same journey, alone or maybe in a shared responsibility, I wanted to share what I had witnessed, what I lived.

And then one therapist, and then a friend, encouraged me to continue writing down my verbal stories.

I shared only from our experiences, only what I hoped would be helpful for a caregiver themselves and their extended support team.

I filled yellow legal pads with scrawled notes of frustrations, tender moments, and life passages. In the dark of night, I scribbled single words on bedside tablets. Later, I journaled on my computer where I recounted My Love's behaviors and my feelings related to my new role. I was fortunate I could capture my thoughts because I could not remember that many details any other way.

I jotted down changing moods and altered behaviors on napkins, on backs of receipts, or wherever I could reference them later. I was able to detect My Love's changes when I looked back through my notes and compared. At first, I wanted to be able to explain unfamiliar situations to My Love's many doctors. So, my notes guided my conversations.

"Now that I am retired, all these diseases show up!" My Love complained. "Why?"

Initially, he was upset to learn of the physical changes going on inside his body. My Love never understood that his years of excessive beer drinking and chain smoking might have seeded his diseases. He had never paid much attention to his father's aging process and his memory loss. Maybe My Love's dementia would not allow him to hear any of it. Regardless of the causes for his memory loss, it was too late.

But the truth was, he never really accepted his changes and kept repeating his life mantra, "I'm keeping a positive attitude; my brain will protect me." Irony.

Losing My Love little by little was not how I anticipated coasting toward the finish line. In my situation, grieving went on even though My Love was still with us.

I felt sadness each time parts of our relationship withered. Sweet invitations to go out stopped appearing on the mirror. Morning wake-up calls announcing our weekend excursions ceased. Conversations dwindled to his immediate needs. As aspects of his personality altered, I mourned. I remained his friend. Those other losses would never return.

Occasionally, I'd sense a tear in his eye, as if he felt what he could not remember. It was not always an outright recognition of a loss, but I wondered if he could *sense the feeling* of that lost memory, if only in a moment of clarity.

I did not always have time for grieving. For me, one sorrow, one loss, just amassed, one upon the other. I imagined one day I would grieve for all my sorrows. But not yet. Changes were happening too quickly. I could hardly keep up, even one-moment-at-a-time. I was still living, breathing, acting in the most important role of my life, caregiver for My Love.

My Love seldom knew when his memories were gone. But I knew. I was the sad one.

Our lives changed, but we could not turn back time!

Journey Note:

"You gain strength, courage and confidence by every experience in which you really stop to look fear in the face. You are able to say to yourself, 'I have lived through this horror. I can take the next thing that comes along.' You must do that thing you think you cannot do."

—Eleanor Roosevelt, *You Learn by Living*: *Eleven Keys for a More Fulfilling Life*

1 MORNING GLORY

Bing!

Toast was up. It needed butter while hot . . . oops, already too late.

I was preparing My Love's tray, as usual, but I took too long, was too slow! And now it was time to turn the eggs over. Reached in the fridge for the juice. Put the carton on the counter. Grabbed the spatula. The dog gave a little whine, and I realized she needed her breakfast . . . just two hours late. Picked up her bowl and put it on the counter beside the juice.

I heard the eggs crackling, edges turning crisp.

On the way toward the stove, I called to My Love. Asked him to feed the dog. My Love couldn't walk to the kitchen fast enough to help. He was confused, in a lot of pain from osteoarthritis in his hip. Plus, he had pains in his legs and groin. Later we found all were from elevated calcium.

Turned stove on low.

I reached into the bag to count out three dog kibbles and dropped them into the dog's bowl. Placed the bowl back on the floor where the dog was sitting patiently. I gave her a little "good girl" pet. Wiped down the counter. Put the dog food bag away.

My Love rounded the corner, walking with a limp. I regretted having called him to move off the couch.

I asked if he wanted a clementine.

Blank response.

I handed him the spatula to turn the eggs.

He asked me why he'd come to the kitchen.

I already fed the dog . . . thought someone needed to watch the eggs, back before I turned them off . . .

But I just said, "Because I am headed to the bathroom and . . ."

As I turned, I flicked the coffee pot on.

Crickets chirping. Incoming text. Grabbed phone from my purse. My son was in the ER in Manchester, saying he was going in for emergency gall bladder surgery. While we were texting, nurses came to get him.

Finally, I hurried down the hall. Put the phone by the bathroom sink. I had to take priority! Used phone to text my daughter so she knew about her brother. Put phone back on the sink counter.

OMG, the phone was ringing! My sister! I hit the button to send that little message that says, "I'll call you later!"

My Love appeared in the bathroom doorway holding the spatula.

"Did you want me to do something with the dog?"

I told My Love I'd get his breakfast and sent him back to the living room.

"Just go back and sit on the couch," I directed.

He handed me the spatula.

Did My Love really just ask about the dog?

He limped back to the couch. I got to the kitchen before he sat down. I filled his plate with food, put it on his tray, and carried it to him just as he finally settled.

But he couldn't put the tray on his lap because his leg muscles were in excessive pain. Rerouted.

I put his tray on the coffee table.

Nooooo! The dog smelled food and headed toward the coffee table.

I swooped up the tray and ran it back to the dining room. I pushed the dog out onto the balcony. Took the tray back to My Love, who forgot his legs hurt long enough to transfer the tray to his tray table!

Oh, juice, you wanted juice or clementine? "Juice, coming right up."

Filled a glass and as I passed the stove, heading for the couch, I cracked another egg. My turn.

"What happened to the eggs?"

I glared at My Love for a moment. "I know the eggs are overcooked, but that's breakfast! Eat it!"

Did I just say that?

Bamboo tone came from my phone to alert me to an incoming email. I glanced at the screen. It said, "Have a happy 76th!"

I silently expressed, *Thank you.* I wondered who would have remembered!

Now, what was I doing?

~

Our mornings had not always simulated a three-ring circus, and I didn't routinely do the kitchen dance, but life was hard to predict when I could not tell the difference between a toddler and my seventy-nine-year-old with dementia.

Maybe the French word *dépaysement,* meaning "to be taken out of a familiar world and placed into a new one, disoriented like a 'fish out of water,' a change of surroundings or scenery," could apply to the life one experienced going through memory loss. I knew, as My Love's caregiver, that there were times I certainly thought that we were living in a bubble somewhere else; maybe in that fish bowl! Definitely, *dépaysement!*

My Love had a form of Alzheimer's disease which was progressing at an unknown rate, on an indefinite schedule, forging an unfamiliar pathway. He also had COPD, vascular dementia, anxiety attacks, and osteoarthritis, and had overcome colon cancer while other mystery diseases were forming. As I stumbled through the bittersweet, I was doing my best to keep up.

What else could happen?

2   FROM THE BEGINNING

My Love's cell phone was ringing.

I noticed he answered it, so I went back to sorting the clothes I just had brought up from the laundry room.

Next thing I knew, he handed his phone to me. Strange. He never did that before.

He leaned in and whispered to me, "It's my doctor."

"Hello, doctor," I said, directing my gaze to My Love for some signal.

I had met My Love's doctor only one time. Did I sound puzzled? *Why does he want to talk to me?*

I sent a silent signal to My Love, lifting my shoulders and raising my eyebrows while shaking my head, hoping he'd understand. My Love stared at me and said nothing.

His doctor began talking about My Love's recent visit, his tests, and then referred to the conclusions. So much all at once. I was trying hard to listen to every word. My Love wandered off, seemingly unaware of the reason his doctor had called.

"I don't understand," I said, a bit curious about the topic. "What tests are we talking about?"

My Love had not mentioned any tests. But then he seldom told me what he did privately. Honestly, I only knew of two doctor visits he had ever mentioned, and neither one was recent.

"Memory tests. I am talking about memory tests," his doctor responded. "Have you noticed any change in his memory lately?"

WOW! Talk about a bomb dropping. Boom!

But then, as a matter of fact, I had noticed My Love's memory failing, a bit. I recalled little things like him forgetting where we'd gone the day before; like forgetting to tell me who had called on the phone; like bringing home eggs instead of bread. He even had forgotten where dishes went in the cabinets. And most of all, conversations sometimes dropped off mid-sentence. I had not been that concerned. We were in our mid-seventies, and a slipping memory was to be expected, wasn't it?

Because My Love had disappeared after handing me his phone, I wondered if he sensed something was going on.

"Well, yes, I have noticed a few little things," I answered the doctor.

Not prepared for the call, I had no examples collected right then. But I had noticed, so maybe I should pay more attention.

"Do you think My Love is going senile?" I asked, not realizing where the doctor's original question would lead! Not even sure what I had just said.

Senile was the term I had heard for those having memory delays at "a certain age." I quickly reminded myself that seniors were known to forget from time to time. My Love was a senior, after all.

The doctor kept talking. "Well, we would like him to take the second set of memory tests. His first ones indicated he could be experiencing mild cognitive impairment; it could be an early sign of dementia. We need to do some investigating to pin down what is going on. Maybe include some other lab testing as well."

I am sure the doctor thought the phone went dead. For a moment I could say nothing. I could not find one word to respond; nothing moved past my lips. For that moment, the conversation had frozen my brain!

"Well, if you think so, then of course," was all I could force myself to say.

That's the best I could say? I thought later. Of course, after the call, my mind flooded with unanswered questions. *When did My Love take those tests? Why didn't he tell me? What will this mean?* I had never heard of mild cognitive impairment. And I knew very little about dementia. *Is that the same as Alzheimer's disease?* And now the doctor was talking about second tests.

My Love's doctor went on. "Perhaps the two of you could come to see me together, and we can talk about what options are ahead."

I felt like I had been scooped up, rebooted, and downloaded into another life, in someone else's bubble, all in the same instant!

My Love and I were going to start seeing his doctor together. Little did we know we'd drive to his doctor's office on a weekly basis for years.

Life ahead? One moment I was independently creating websites, working in my own business, thinking that was what I would be doing for a few more years. Then in the next moment, I felt like I would be nowhere near a computer, wholly disconnected from designing. We were on that moving sidewalk of life and had just been shunted in a new direction. Clunk!

My Love might have dementia! Even Alzheimer's disease!

I was entirely out of my comfort zone. A sense of real fear went through my body. Was I shaking? I felt wobbly, ungrounded.

What do I do now?

By then I had taken My Love's phone and gone out onto the balcony to be alone as I arranged an appointment date and finished up the conversation with his doctor.

~

"Have you noticed any memory loss?" the doctor had asked me during his call. "With your loved one," he added.

I did not realize the increased number of times My Love's slipping memory was a clue that something bigger than just turning seventy-five was going on in his brain. He always said he felt good!

When anyone suggested he was aging, My Love would puff out his chest and say, "Oh, I still have the body of a Greek god! I am fine!"

But lately, his chest had been gradually shrinking in size with the rest of his body. He measured four inches shorter than when we met. He was more than fifty pounds lighter.

But over time, my standard response had become short, "Good to hear!"

Reviewing the doctor's concerns, I realized, yes, My Love may have been in great shape at one time, but things were changing. Age and a new illness were taking its toll on him. I suspected his inner child was never going to allow him to admit to any physical decline, let alone memory loss.

~

My Love was tapping his fingers on the small desk in the examination room. The doctor had finished explaining My Love's disease and was beginning to outline our new future. Hoping there would be no more discussion about his memory, or loss of it, My Love stood to leave.

"So, are we done here?" he asked the doctor as he looked at me and nodded toward the door, impatiently waiting for me to stand and follow.

I didn't.

I could not seem to move my gaze from the blood pressure cuff that hung on the wall. I did not hear the doctor answer "yes" as he stood and left the room. I did not see the nurse come in to straighten up the examination table. I did not even hear the paper crinkle as I vaguely watched her pull on a smooth, new section.

But she got my attention when she put her hand on my shoulder and asked, "Are you all right, honey?"

I gave my head a shake. Honey put on a smile and grabbed My Love's hand and together we walked out of the doctor's office. Breathe!

It wasn't long before I accepted there would be no more designing, no more websites, no new company logos, nor client meetings. No content editing. I would pack up my marketing hat and put away my writer's sketchbook. I was donning the garb of a student learning about a second baffling disease. I had never felt so depressed. And it was only one hour since diagnosis!

~

I liked learning new things, but the subjects usually were of my choosing. Alzheimer's disease had never made it onto the list of areas I chose to study. I wanted to learn watercolor painting and maybe join the weaving guild at the art gallery. I had to sort the piles of books stacked by my couch, begging to share their magic. Perhaps I'd surprise my kids and take a cooking class.

For sure, I planned to play my autoharp and learn more than three notes on my dulcimer, as soon as my trigger fingers healed and the swelling in my hands and wrists subsided.

But instead, learning about Alzheimer's disease leaped to the top of my to-do list. My monkey mind was at work; my thoughts were jumping all over, coming at me from all directions. I needed time to sort out what had just happened.

But there was no time. Life was carrying on whether we were ready or not. Diseases were progressing. My Love and I wanted to know what lay ahead of us.

I began to feel like the family pioneer, scouting ahead to see what was out there. I just didn't know where I was going.

Knowing scientists studied these diseases, I thought about going to our nearby university to see someone in their medical system. I made a note to call. My confusion was clouding my thought process.

Who should I talk to?

None of our friends were experiencing memory loss. I was not aware of any older friends who had parents with dementia. I had not paid attention. Here we were, the age of grandparents and we didn't know anyone with dementia or Alzheimer's disease. Very fortunate, I thought. Or a huge, well-kept secret.

Who could I talk to?

I knew of no one in my family who had ever been diagnosed with memory loss. My Love's twin brother had no known dementia issues. Maybe their father had lost some memory just before he died. Even so, My Love had not been ill before he retired. Well, change was in the air.

Who was I going to talk to?

As always in my life, the Universe knew I needed help. Support was on the way!

My thoughts were fuzzy. At no time had it crossed my mind to look for a health charity organization where there might be information and guidance. Originally, I felt guided to look for a phone book, the thick Yellow Pages. Surely, lots of Alzheimer's names would be listed! But, of course, we no longer had a big yellow phone book! Not for years! The Universe needed to catch up!

I would have to ask Google to find our answer. There were hundreds of sites returned when I entered "Alzheimer's" into the search field on the internet.

Of course! Even though I was unfamiliar with Alzheimer's disease, Google had been collecting the most current information for years, just waiting for my search.

I found information on the Canadian Alzheimer Society website. They expressed that over half a million people in Canada were living with dementia in 2018. The expectation for 2031 was one million. Of that number, two-thirds were women. Moreover, more than twenty-five thousand new cases each year were diagnosed.

I read on the Alzheimer Association site that 6.2 million people in all of North America were living with dementia.

The Dementia Australia site published, "#Every3Seconds someone globally develops dementia."

Staggering statistics!

Still, My Love and I could not think of one person we knew.

I found an Alzheimer Association. I noted the word Alzheimer's showed up in many countries, listed with events, organizations, paraphernalia, and provincial groups related to Alzheimer's disease. The listings seemed endless. Sites existed about any aspect of Alzheimer's I wanted to know. It was Google, after all.

So, I tweaked my search to Alzheimer Ontario. And reliable Google brought up the Alzheimer Society of Ontario.

While scrolling through the rest of the search page, I noted many site addresses related to care of those with Alzheimer's disease in Ontario. And then I added our town name to the search. Up came the Alzheimer Society of the regions, including ours. Ah-ha! Jotting their contact information onto a scrap of paper got me started.

To keep the momentum going, I phoned their local office immediately.

Unbelievable!

"Can we help you?" came across the phone.

"Yes! I hope you can!" I answered. Our relationship began with my call.

Someone was there. It was four o'clock on a Friday afternoon, but they could help me!

Not only did they have pamphlets to help me learn, but they also had someone there to talk to me right away. They would begin by explaining to me all the ways they could help both of us going forward. It was the most remarkable feeling of relief to realize the emotional weight sitting on my shoulders had just floated away. I felt a sigh of gratefulness deep inside. I knew I would have a safety net, real support.

Only days after learning of our life change, I had found someone to talk to and had discovered where I would learn much more. I only had to make the appointment and get to their office.

I had taken that first step.

~

It turned out that the Alzheimer Society would become a steady hand, an enduring calm, to reassure us during our unbelievable journey. And we could drive to their office in twenty minutes or connect by phone any time.

I discovered they offered classes for couples. Through their programs, we were given opportunities to meet others in similar situations, to have educational discussions for facing unknowns. Their caring staff were ready to help. I sensed I would visit them often! Deep breath!

I had no idea what my new role would be. We didn't prepare for things we didn't expect to happen. I didn't.

After browsing, I found that our Society's branch office housed a library of literature covering many issues and that their Monthly Cafés, held in a roundtable format, existed for getting answers in a Q&A setting. I even discovered professional counselors were on staff to help with personal questions and, as I would find invaluable later, with planning strategies.

To me, *memory loss* meant complicated times, stress and emotions, and hours of unfamiliar behaviors were ahead. Thank goodness those Alzheimer Society folks had answers ready for newbies like My Love and me! I never dreamed I would find encouragement right away.

Fortunate!

If My Love was going to have some rotten, nasty, incurable disease, terrible as it sounded, this was the one! All kinds of support would be available! I could begin to sleep nights!

The Alzheimer Society of our region is not part of the federal or provincial government. The Society's existence relies mainly on public funding, donations made surrounding their Annual Walks, and yearly contributions from individual donors, corporations, communities, and foundations. We participated and contributed.

The most compassionate, understanding, intelligent, helpful, and kind human beings on the planet chose to share their unique talents with the Alzheimer Society and with us, their clients. Volunteers with similar qualities were drawn to stay with them year after year. Best of all, no one needed a doctor's referral to become a client or to use their services.

Even though we were just getting involved, I felt good knowing professionals would be there to walk the walk with us. I was happy I had sought out the Alzheimer Society; I was grateful I had been guided to take the step!

3 CAREGIVER

"Is there any ice cream?"

I heard those words breaking through my train of thought, jolting me back to My Love's request coming from the kitchen. On his new diet, he ate dairy-free ice cream. Coconut and cashew had become a habit-forming passion. I did try to hide it deep in the freezer, or he'd consume the whole small, priced-like-gold container in one sitting.

Didn't he finish two cookies a few minutes ago?

No matter what dietary constraints I tried to follow, he'd find something to crave any time of day. It was characteristic for loved ones with Alzheimer's disease to graze; My Love fit the description, to the extreme. He searched for cookies, chips, and ice cream all day long. I kept nutrition drinks in the fridge to be sure there were vitamins and minerals in his diet somewhere. We even kept protein bars and dried cereal in the car console. It seemed unfair, but his slim body never gained an ounce.

When My Love asked, "Have we had breakfast yet?" it began to sound like kids nagging, "Are we there yet?"

"Did you hide the cookies?" he asked, hoping I had forgotten to show him more to eat.

By then I would hear him searching through the refrigerator, even after breakfast was over. He could see the dishes were washed up, drying in the drainer. I knew that meant nothing. He searched all day, like a restless youngster, except My Love was a somewhat sedentary, seventy-nine-year-old snack-a-holic.

He made trips to the kitchen regardless of the hour.

"It's ten minutes to five. When is dinner?"

His question was as regular as his wristwatch, which he religiously checked around the clock. Depending on the minute, he announced the time for the dog walks, dog meals, departure for classes and doctor appointments, getting the mail, his medicines, our scheduled meals, *M.A.S.H.*, and his bedtime!

"Is it already suppertime?" I asked, clearly oblivious to the hour. "Let's do pizza first, then I'll find your ice cream," I responded with a sense of guilt, knowing I had been typing far too long.

Still, experience had taught me My Love would be thrilled that for at least one day that week, he would not have to wait an hour while I prepared a home-cooked meal.

~

Not so long ago I had no idea I'd be a caregiver. The role just evolved as the need became evident. No one asked if I wanted to do it. I had never committed to taking care of My Love "in sickness and in health." I never aspired to give up my life for someone else.

Where would I find patience, compassion, or understanding? I didn't have the necessary skills or knowledge. But there never seemed to be a choice.

If not me, who? kept sneaking into my conflicted thoughts.

As I closed my eyes, and half-heartedly gave in, I silently prayed, *Please, dear God, help me do this.*

And just like that, I was a caregiver.

Evidently, God had agreed to my prayer, one I might later wish I had not uttered. I gave one last attempt to wiggle out. Looking for excuses, I confessed, *I don't know what I'm supposed to do.*

With an intention to overcome my fear and put aside my ego, and with a fervent hope that I could find the love and grace I knew I would need along the way, I carried on, preparing to face both happiness and despair, the bittersweet that was to come.

My Love's illnesses superseded everything else in our lives and became my full-time focus. Memories that tethered him to reality were dissolving. Recollections of his skiing days, his boating years, his business life, his current daily activities, and even his family seemed to be splitting into fragments. His coughing and anxiety flare-ups were increasing, sometimes day by day. His breathing difficulties came and went.

No alternative solution appeared. Secretly terrified, I assumed the role permanently.

I often re-read my journey journals about My Love's illnesses. As I did, it became crystal clear how, in a sliver of time, I had glided invisibly through the gap, as if I were a stowaway on Will Smith and Jeff Goldblum's alien spaceship in the movie *Independence Day*. A gap between who-I-thought-I-was and who-I-was-becoming narrowed as I emerged into the caregiver role. Was I witnessing, through my writing, the entrance of that nurturing compassion that I had consciously resisted fifty years earlier?

My Love seemed to have no one else who would care for him. The heavy burden of being responsible for another human being kept troubling me to the depths of my soul. My heart was in agony.

I genuinely don't want to do this. I keep saying it, but I really don't!

When I was alone, I kept longing for an angel of salvation to whisk me away to some other reality.

It's not fair! I had plans for my retirement! I worked for my golden years!

But no rescue came.

Shame on me. I know this man needs me. Why do I want to get away?

I could not quiet my thoughts. Having My Love's life solely in my hands was a terrifying prospect.

Is this really a calling? Will I miss my calling if I ignore this moment at this unexpected crossroad?

The thoughts flashed across my mind. His needs were facing me straight on. My choice was inevitable. Filled with uncertainty, I followed the call.

Soon, weeks turned into months and then years. I learned what stamina was. I found out what commitment meant. I experienced how burnout felt. Some called it compassion fatigue. I called it flat-out exhaustion!

~

And then, when I heard John Denver and Placido Domingo singing Denver's "Perhaps Love," I recognized I was experiencing the love that binds us to one another as human beings. While writing my stories about how challenging my new tasks were, I felt a subtle transformation. In addition to explaining my caregiving activities, I found I was talking about human reactions, emotions. I was uncovering my innermost caregiver.

I finally felt the distinction that helped me appreciate how important my role would be. Where would this new awareness lead me?

~

For a brief time in college, I considered the possibility of becoming a nurse. I thought briefly about joining that honorable, caring profession that focused on responsiveness to the well-being of others. I looked at some of the course titles.

Responsibility for Adults
Science of Nursing Practice
Philosophy of Bioethics
Responsibility for Children

None resonated. In the end, I pushed back from a career where I would need to tend to others, day in, day out. Nurturing did not ignite any sparks within back then. Furthermore, I was not a student gifted in the sciences. Was that an excuse? I could not imagine a life where I'd give full-time care as a nurse, the medical profession for women in my time. No. Nursing was not for me, especially not during those years, when my health was of concern.

During my college years, I had an autoimmune neuromuscular disease, myasthenia gravis (MG). Although not diagnosed until I was eighteen years old, I had had it since I was twelve. I went through the two semesters of my freshman year undiagnosed. It was not until the middle of the fall of my second year that the disease was identified. Then, twenty-one years later, when I was almost thirty-nine, MG began to go into remission, though it never entirely left my body nor my mind.

In the interest of understanding the impact myasthenia gravis had on my life, and throughout my caregiver role, I share brief explanations in layman's terms.

The distinguishing characteristic of myasthenia gravis is muscle weakness that worsens after periods of activity and improves after periods of rest. Apparently, between 1956 and 1961, the broader medical community began seriously researching myasthenia gravis, which until then was an unstudied and little-known disease. Was it a coincidence that those were the same years my family was searching for a diagnosis for my weakened condition?

Every day during those years, living with myasthenia gravis was a physical challenge. Although my leg and arm muscles seemed the most affected, my eyelids drooped and my vision blurred. My breathing muscles and lungs weakened, frequently without warning. At times my speech slurred and I had trouble swallowing. All muscles were affected in some way.

Basically, "call-to-action" messages were not getting from my brain to my muscles.

Daily, I was exhausted. My muscles ached as I awkwardly struggled to walk or climb stairs. Myasthenia limited my power to move. I would pull myself up the steps with my arms holding the railing or fingers grasping at the wall, Spiderman style. Being unsteady, I needed support and sometimes an umbrella substituted for a cane. Often, I had no strength to carry even a paperback book. Plus, how could I read it when my eyelids strained to stay open? Many books went unread. Often, I was sure I felt brain fatigue, like my brain was struggling to think.

As a college freshman, I was looking forward to a new and positive life. It was hard to be negative or to brood over limitations when I was excited to get out on my own and live. But physical activity, even at eighteen years old, was not easy. Only I knew the effort it took to take each step, to move any limb, to focus my eyes, to do anything physical. Thus, I tried to plan my days in strategic ways.

Back then, I could not take care of anyone but myself, and even that was unpredictable. So, with my chin up, I dismissed the idea of nursing and carried on with my class schedules while searching for a college course of study, something I'd want to practice for the rest of my life.

That was 1960. Life was slower then. Sitting here in 2018 it is incredible to see the changes in nearly six decades. Back then, in our three-story walk-up university dormitory, I had to walk down to the lobby to use the phone, a pay-phone in a wood and glass phone booth. Our newspapers were available in the lobby dispensers. We did get local radio reception, but I don't recall a television in the building.

I borrowed my roommate's heavy Underwood standard typewriter to finalize typed reports. Most papers were handwritten. I availed myself of a desk model Sperry Remington adding machine in the business building if I needed it. No hand-held calculators had been developed yet. In our college town, we used buses to get around. But on campus, traveling on foot was the norm. I was at the mercy of my legs and feet. We'd have to wait forty years for a Segway transporter!

There were no cell phones. No computers. No electronic tablets. No internet. No Google. We had no Wi-Fi. We did not sit at a desk in the library hooked to the internet, downloading into our laptop or tablet all the information we needed to complete our homework. Instead, we climbed through the stacks, using information from the card catalogs—created from the Dewey decimal system, a sort of "ancient" GPS system—to locate our information. And then, of course, we had to copy what we wanted by hand into a notebook. At least, I knew no other way then.

My activity choices were based on what I could do physically and how much time I needed to do it. How far could I walk or climb without pain? How many books could I carry in a bag? How many pages could I read before my eyes drooped too far? How many notes could I write before my hands would cramp and could no longer grasp a pencil?

I learned various ways to hold that little yellow stick with least pain because I practiced. I wanted to be a writer or a storyteller. In fact, at that time, I wanted to be a journalist more than anything. Not a reporter exactly, but a writer, a communicator, living and working and socializing amid the hustle and bustle of the news-writing crowd.

In the late 1950s, I was fortunate to have been chosen to be a feature writer on *The Owl*, our historic high school newspaper that started as a magazine in

1908 and first published as a newspaper in 1920. I loved every minute "soaring with the Owls." I presumed a journalism degree would give me more of that same atmosphere. But to get there, I had to become a reporting journalist, walking, talking, writing. Or so I thought.

With myasthenia gravis, it was difficult to be mobile. I could hardly walk across the street. I spent lots of time calculating class schedules to find the shortest route, with the fewest stairs, and the least walking time to and from classes. I needed to generate the least pain and still be on time. I was fortunate the Liberal Arts buildings were on the near side of campus.

After a year, I started to give in. It became obvious to me I probably could never become a journalist because I could not walk very well. Certainly, I could not go "scoop the action." How would I get anywhere, on or off campus, to investigate newsworthy leads, to confirm information, or even to find topics for feature articles, with my own obstacles in play? Just on campus. Still, I wanted to write. I kept taking courses. But, in the end, after the second year, I had to let go of my dream. A journalism degree was not going to be in my future.

Even though I was taking basic college courses, I had to get serious about picking my major subject if I wanted to graduate. I wondered if I could become an accountant. They never had to walk anywhere, did they? I could sit at a desk. Of course, I might need to learn math again; I never did well with numbers, even with the help of my fingers. And hand-held adding machines were still just a germ of an idea.

During high school, through the Junior Achievement program, I had been a bank teller during the summers. During my university years, I was fortunate to have had the support of the JA sponsor and the bank manager to enable me to continue earning funds for college expenses.

Although I was working with figures and money, that was as close to bookkeeping as I wanted to be. I never intended banking to be a career. I was not sure why I thought I could do bookkeeping at all!

Was it that cute accounting student attending the sign-up desk at registration who first got my interest and who then processed my paperwork?

Hormones and insanity!

I tried one beginner's bookkeeping class for one month and dropped out. I finally grasped that bookkeeping would not be my profession. My brain could not wrap around the basic idea of debits and credits. Mental block? Maybe. To this day I freeze in terror thinking how life would have been if I had pursued that profession, one where others seem to thrive. So, my final interest to consider was art. It met the criteria I was developing: no exhaustive physical activity, no science, no math. I had always loved art. "Basket weaving," my first husband called it.

As it turned out, I loved all my art classes. I loved being with artists, sharing thoughts and ideas, and being absorbed in the different media and class projects each semester; every minute resonated. Labs and classes, theory and history. And, yes, basket weaving!

I felt at home with the smell of turpentine and oil paints. My eyes danced at the chance to pick colors and soft yarns for weaving. In the pottery room, squishing slurry between my fingers while working with clay made me feel like a kid playing in the mud. Those same hands and fingers loved caressing the wood I carved and sanded smooth as glass. Art felt right.

I loved sitting at the drawing tables with paper and pencil, sketching ideas before proceeding outside to bring them to life in full color. The library books I browsed were like finding treasures. I learned what I could about artists. I was like a sponge when I listened to lectures, or immersed myself in lab projects, or studied shows displayed in the galleries. It was a joy to have classes in the Fine Arts building.

Once content with the idea of an art degree, it did not matter what I intended to do with it following graduation. I was hooked on art. I loved talking with the art professors who taught us, plus the artists who visited their classes. I still love art classes. Stress release!

So, I chose to study art. I spent my last three years in university as an art student and got my Bachelor of Arts degree in Art. Of course, then I had to take quite a few more classes to get my teaching certificate! But I was finally able to get out on my own!

With my writing profession in the tank along with short-lived bookkeeping and nursing considerations, an art-teaching career was to be my life. And it was the basis for an extraordinary existence, and a remarkable professional career, in all sorts of ways.

After teaching art in middle school and high school on the Navajo Reservation in New Mexico, I taught in a kindergarten while my husband studied for his PhD at Texas A&M University. There, a dear friend and I owned a gift shop of consigned artwork and handmade goods, all originals. When our family moved to a larger city, I stepped into the unfamiliar oil-field corporate world, beginning as an untested advertising coordinator. For twenty-seven years, I worked with several exhibit design/build firms in the US and Canada. With experience, I became a marketing manager. Finally, I designed for clients through my own website design business, until after

I "retired." I owe a big thank you to my well-chosen Arts degree. But at no time was I a caregiver, ever.

Even with myasthenia gravis, and my relationship with the medical field, the idea of caregiving rarely, if ever, crossed my mind!

So, when, in my first Alzheimer Society class, I asked, "What does a caregiver do?" I honestly wasn't sure. When I said I had no training to be a caregiver, except being a parent, I was not acting flippant.

But, of course, I had had training. My whole life I'd been preparing, building up my repertoire of ingenuity and know-how. Being a parent, especially a single parent for a time, had just been life moments along the way.

I would have to muster up every talent I ever practiced and all the understanding I ever gathered while caring for my family, and then expand it all into imaginative strategies to become a caregiver.

But the universe, as always, showed me what was right for me. This time was no different.

Through rewriting my story, I found where my new understanding of caregiving would take me. I had succeeded in going full circle to become the person I was so sure I could not, so adamant I would not, become. A caregiver.

~

The point was, even though I did not become a journalist, I still was a writer. And in those waning years of bitter and sweet, I felt compelled to tell My Love's stories; I could be a writer and at the same time become a caregiver.

In my classes, it had become obvious that there were going to be obstacles, hurdles, and stumbling blocks. I would have to face them, and erase them, to carry on my caregiving tasks. Think: super-woman!

Finally, one morning while in the shower, where I seemed to do a lot of serious self-talk, where I gave my best silent soliloquies, I felt I was being niggled about understanding caregiving versus caregiver.

As the streams of warm water tapped down on my head, I sensed my inner caregiver beginning to stir. I realized that it would be through a *caregiving caregiver* that I would relate our stories of surviving the plaques and tangles misbehaving in My Love's brain. I wanted my stories to act as encouragement for caregivers, letting them know the moments ahead could be both frustrating and rewarding; distressing, yet full of emotions that would range from distress, anger, and aggression to love, joy, humor, and, yes, heartache.

Most importantly, I had to stress to caregivers the importance of finding lifelines to hold onto throughout their journey.

4   ALZHEIMER'S WORLD

Alzheimer's and hope.

How could two words make such a difference in our lives?

"Are you doing ok?" a friend asked me after hearing My Love had vascular dementia and Alzheimer's disease, knowing it meant substantial life adjustments.

"It's all about **HOPE**," I told her. "**H**ave **O**ne **P**ositive **E**xperience." A phrase I had recently learned from a local Alzheimer's support group.

It was so perfect for me because I generally tried to keep a spark of hope, a sense of something positive coming just around the next corner. I did want to remain positive, after all.

"At first, I pretended dementia wasn't part of our lives. I couldn't imagine that My Love would eventually lose his memories! But he did!" I admitted. "Once I started learning, taking classes, I understood more. I met new friends. I needed lots of support. I am grateful for the hope I received."

I trusted others would realize that, along with education, daily hope was important.

~

So much to learn! Right away I found education classes at the Alzheimer Society, where I was exposed to all that lay ahead. My Love and I signed up for an overview class that included legal aspects, family expectations, and health and diet advice.

One of the couples we met in our first class became part of the Lifeliner Group that evolved a couple of years later. Walking their talk, the Alzheimer Society encouraged social interaction from the very beginning.

In more specific courses we were introduced to the physiological characteristics and the psychological implications of the various dementia diseases, of which Alzheimer's disease is only one.

Later there would be social events, comprehensive education classes, creative groups, and counseling sessions in which we would become involved as a couple and as individuals. In addition, the Society put folks in touch with helpful local services beyond the Society's scope. Support beyond belief.

First, I learned dementia was not a specific disease, but a broad term used to describe a set of symptoms that involved a form of mental impairment, such as memory loss, confusion, or personality changes. Examples of dementia explained were far more than the Alzheimer's disease and vascular dementia of My Love's diagnosis. Be sure to contact your medical professional or a nearby Alzheimer Society office for further guidance and discussion on the various dementia diseases. There are numerous online sites where more information is given. I am only a caregiver. I do not want to lead anyone astray; talk to your health care providers.

With tears in my eyes, during a class break, I hid my face and whispered to the facilitator, "I don't think I will be able to do this."

She wrapped her arm around me. "Yes, you will."

She squeezed my shoulders and then went back to the podium.

No one knew how alone I felt nor how much my life ahead terrified me at that moment.

Caregiving responsibilities presented a heavy load. I understood I would be carrying on, mostly alone. My Love's family members, although not too far away, were otherwise committed and rarely involved. My family lived in another country. Our friends had dropped away over time. Some seemed uncomfortable being associated with a person with dementia. Some were getting older themselves.

Some found nothing in common with someone who did not drink anymore. But I had faced challenges all my life. To me, challenges meant making mind shifts, modifying my thinking and actions. With any luck, this would be no different! The facilitator was right. One step at a time, taking my new world in little by little, I would be able to be a caregiver.

Knowing who to call with questions built up my confidence. In time, we began fitting in and accepting Alzheimer's world, the sphere of so many we had recently met.

In Alzheimer's group gatherings, I heard heart-warming stories about good times each week. On the other hand, it was a challenge to listen to those caregivers whose every effort was a struggle. I sympathized with their agony, but I had to be careful not to take the negative energy home.

I tried to remember the fundamental physiology and symptoms of all dementia, plus My Love's non-dementia illnesses. I was not ready for so much. I didn't know where to put my attention. Was I getting a medical certificate? Thank goodness all My Love's doctors were taking care of medical knowledge.

I found more about Alzheimer's disease on the Alzheimer Society of Canada website, _www.alzheimer._ _ca_: "Normal aging vs. dementia: Alzheimer's disease and other dementias are not a part of normal aging.

. . . When there is no underlying medical condition causing this memory loss, it is known as 'age-associated memory impairment,' which is considered a part of the normal aging process."

The Alzheimer Society website added:

"Behaviors associated with complex and challenging mental health, dementia or other neurological conditions include aggression, wandering and agitation. These apparent changes in the personality of the person with the disease are a major source of distress both to the person who is presenting the behaviors and to those who experience them– the caregiver, the family members, and the service providers in all sectors of the health-care system."

We learned strategies that were known to help in memory loss scenarios. If "A" happened, we could try certain tactics. If "B" happened, try something else. I could not remember everything, but I wrote down the phone numbers and email addresses of people who knew approaches and who had indicated they had dealt with specific situations.

I collected brochures and pamphlets and put them in a notebook. I downloaded articles that seemed appropriate and read them at different times. When it became too much, I learned to revisit those topics later, at a more relevant time. What I hoped to do when the time arrived, a time when I needed a certain aspect of the information, was to make the appropriate contact. I hoped the specialists would be there to call upon when I needed them.

My resource binder was bulging. My brain could take no more. Sometimes I talked with My Love about what I was learning. He had little interest and rarely listened.

But one time while talking with My Love soon after his diagnosis, I included, just as a fact in a conversation and without having much more information to explain, "It could happen that as we age, we might have to move to a long-term care home."

"Are you kidding? I would never live in any other home but ours," he snapped. "If you mention that again, I just might throw you over the balcony."

What a strange response. He wasn't laughing. I wondered which words had touched off a nerve. I had no warning. He'd never been that sensitive about anything. A new and sudden change in his behavior got my attention.

In his anger, he picked up a dining room chair and launched it toward me across the living room. I knew the moment it left his hands he realized he didn't mean to do it, but he had done it. His swift reaction surprised me! Instinctively, I took a picture.

He was far stronger than I was. My Love's reaction was so terrible, so scary for me, that I vowed it would be years before I spoke to him about long-term care again.

I lived with my "alert" button turned on thereafter, waiting for another violent moment. I could handle rough, maybe aggressive, but not violent. Later, I wondered if his high calcium had been the trigger. Anyone feeling cornered, maybe betrayed, as he might have felt, would surely lash out. That incident had been two years before we knew about the calcium. Still, it had happened. He had thrown the chair. I remained cautious and vigilant throughout our remaining time together.

And then, one day I awoke and just knew life would be ok. Finally. I knew I did not have to soak up every word I had heard in class. The right responses would come to me. I had sufficient knowledge at my fingertips; all of it did not need to be in my brain. I had the names and phone numbers of countless people who could prompt my memory for the answers I had filed away . . . I just didn't know where. Resources!

I took the first step. And then a second. Support was there!

So, when asked how we were doing, I wanted to shout from the stars. I was excited to find so many caring people in the many related local health and charity organizations who understood what we were going through. I was grateful for the compassionate, caring, knowledgeable professionals who had been working with caregivers and loved ones, who were there for us.

There for us and for me, the caregiver!

Yes, at first I was terrified when we took the turn toward Alzheimer's world. But when I found resources and help, I predicted we would be fine. When I reached out, I breathed easier when I felt a helping hand reach back with hope.

Finally, a good feeling!

 5   NOTES

"Who can remember all this?" I asked the attending technician during the Memory Clinic visit when I first accompanied My Love. "Was I supposed to bring an eighteen-month history?"

That time I heard a bit of snark in my voice.

I could sense I was falling deeper into anxiety. I had no notes, I was just learning the lingo. This consultation was my first visit as caregiver. I did not know what signs or indicators to watch for in My Love's life during those early months of dementia. I was learning at that meeting about the clinic, their procedures, and the tests he had taken. I soon learned taking notes would have been a good idea.

My Love went to four of such clinics in four years, including his first one, the year before he was first diagnosed.

I always thought that evaluation was more to repeat tests, so the doctors could compare My Love's current status to the baseline tests he had taken initially, not to test my memory of what happened over the year.

However, I learned I was to be included in the questioning. The doctors were going to use what I said, plus My Love's new test scores, to determine his changes from the last visit. They did give us a brief verbal recap of the results of our visit. In my state of stress, I did not recall much. Thank goodness written details went to his family doctor.

The questions they asked me caught me off guard.

"How many times do you think he . . .?"

Who keeps count?

"When does he mostly act like . . .?"

Good grief, who knows?

"What did you do when he behaved that way?"

Was it longer than a week ago? Then I have no recollection because too much has clouded that memory over with new ones this week.

I felt like I was being grilled, that I was the one having a memory test, all because I had no notes for our appointment.

Wonder if they noted my annoyed responses in their records?

I kept thinking I must have missed where the class leader suggested caregivers keep track or record situational changes for future reference. That had to be back when I was still drowning in information overload.

At least I know what to anticipate next time.

In my new world, I just was too exhausted to keep taking notes in detail.

Why don't I know shorthand?

Furthermore, by each new day, we were facing different issues. I kept notes on important events, not daily tasks. Then even those events took too much time to record.

On that first visit, I was not prepared to answer the clinic's questions that depended on my memory. (That wasn't going to happen again!) I told them what I could remember, mentioning eighteen months was a very long time! Lots could change. The past was gone.

Did they hear that?

The doctor and memory specialist both were patient with me, a kindness that gave me mental space to consider what would be helpful for the next time.

Following that morning at the clinic, I decided to keep a specific journal. I knew it would be easier to reflect over eighteen months with reference notes! I just had to begin another new habit.

Google helped me find the perfect journal program. I began using it immediately. The practice seemed to defuse apprehensions. By exposing my observations and worries, I, at least, had acknowledged them.

My words and visions downloaded through my brain-pipe to my fingertips, which seemed to come awake the moment my hands hovered over a keyboard. Nothing really seemed conscious about the process until I read the words that came alive across the screen, the moment I became involved. Strange.

I could chronicle activities, behaviors, responses, and unusual experiences. I created a special page just for noting questions for My Love's doctor and for the memory clinic, all from one program. The perfect solution. I knew my notes were there, by date, for future use.

Who would have imagined that one year later I would print out seventeen pages for the memory clinic? Well, no, I did not take seventeen pages. I condensed them. In so doing, I had to read through them. I was grateful to have information I would never have recalled and especially not in such detail.

I chuckled after the first appointment when I took my recap for the clinic technician's file. She didn't want them! No one wanted those notes! What a world. They had been for me.

Just the same, I was glad I had kept notes. I was even happier I had read them recently. And in the end, I realized I was the one who really could see the distance we had covered in the past twelve months. My journal program became an essential tool as I wrote even more notes.

6   BURIED TREASURE

"The memory tests you took confirm you have Alzheimer's disease, one of the dementia diseases," My Love's doctor was explaining to My Love and me, as he looked up briefly from his computer screen.

He was recapping the results of the second set of tests, directing his comments toward his patient, My Love.

Although the doctor had mentioned Alzheimer's disease earlier, I realized I had not been paying attention to My Love. I was conflicted to hear the doctor's words. I wanted to know, yet I didn't. I kept listening, waiting for the big picture, the "how we're going to fix it" highpoint of his diagnosis.

Seeing no reaction from My Love, nor from me, the doctor went on. "The tests confirm you have a brain disorder. Your ability to carry out your daily activities will be affected from now on." The doctor paused.

We can't fix it?

I realized I wasn't ready to hear that!

"The results indicate a combination disease known as mixed dementia, the name assigned when more than one type of memory loss occurs at the same time in the brain."

He must have thought we understood. He just kept speaking; he did not look up. But I was lost, and my Love seemed in a daze, way too calm.

"Let me catch up," I stopped the doctor, raising my hands like a traffic cop. "You said mixed dementia? My Love has memory loss from more than one disease?" I quizzed, reaching for my stomach.

"Yes, it seems from two separate dementia diseases. It is not uncommon for those with memory loss to have more than one of the dementia diseases. It all depends which lobes of the brain are affected. Different diseases cause separate behaviors. We'll get one more test to confirm vascular dementia." His doctor added, "But the recent tests pointed to Alzheimer's disease with indicators of vascular dementia."

Hearing words Alzheimer's disease and dementia, I could sense an uneasiness surging up my legs, through to my pounding heart. I couldn't hold back the tears sitting on the edges of my eyes, about to fall onto my cheeks. I had heard the doctor say those words when we spoke on the phone but hearing the words in person made them absolute.

That was the first time in years that I felt my stomach churning, the butterflies of panic.

I watched My Love sit there, arms across his chest, seeming to wait for me to speak. I couldn't be sure he even heard what the doctor had said. Perhaps he did not want to put a name to something he might have felt inside for a long time. He just stared.

It was later when I realized identifying dementia might have been too much for My Love to grasp, even in those early stages of memory loss. Could he have felt fear upon hearing the words? Could dread have blocked his brain from receiving the information? Was he retreating inside to a safe zone? Could he really understand?

~

I began to sense that caregiving was going to be both a blessing and a curse. Although it was an unsettling decision, I half-heartedly renewed my commitment to our future. But, surprising to me, something about my untested role was starting to transform my understanding of care. Was this role going to be a gift? Was I going to become a caring human being after all?

I was unaware of any innate skills I possessed for caregiving. I just happened to see through a window to wisdom that had been put before me for one brief moment. I saw me being a caring person.

I sensed something happen from the depths of my soul, pushing against my outward resistance. Had I touched upon that buried treasure, that intense feeling of compassion that Deepak Chopra mentioned in *The Book of Secrets, Unlocking the Hidden Dimension of Your Life*?

Maybe, for that one brief moment.

And then, there were those days when I wanted to walk away, wanted to get out from under the anticipated agony! Why did I have to do this? Did anyone ask if I wanted the job? Who else had offered to do this?

~

I glanced at the man I had spent years with, my friend, My Love. I realized our life was changing, and I had to get my head around our future.

As the doctor's words became clear, I understood My Love now had a second incurable disease. The first, COPD, was one I still knew very little about. Now I had to learn even more.

What more do I need to study? Why me? What should I do? Do I have to do this? I asked myself, but I had no answer.

I realized I was looking at our life through entirely new lenses. I saw My Love's small forgetful moments take on new meaning.

More than a few times, I felt like I was the only one who cared.

Then I'd close my eyes and scream inside as loudly as I could, *I don't want to be a caregiver!*

Breathe.

No one ever heard me. And incredible as it was, my caregiving had only just begun! Because writing had been my automatic go-to for relief, I acknowledged it became essential to have reference notes. There was too much to remember.

Often, I wondered if I were catching his "forgetting" disease. The Alzheimer Society had assured me that dementia was not contagious, so I just kept jotting down questions, looking for answers.

Questions never quite answered were:

-How did My Love sleep at night with his diseases? My Love never liked to talk about his illnesses, only his immediate pains. In fact, he didn't think he had any illnesses. He slept well, rarely exhibiting any outward stress about his diseases he didn't believe he had.

-With all those horrible diseases, what was My Love feeling inside? I never knew. The farther we were from diagnosis, the less likely I would ever know his inner thoughts, especially from one who never

talked about emotions, one who thought the doctors were wrong, anyway.

-*Was I making the best choices for My Love?* It was a painful burden to have the life of another in my hands, wholly in my hands! Every day, tough decisions.

Every night, I tossed for sleepless hours. He slept quite soundly as long as the dog and I were in the room, in the bed, sleeping.

I logged into my journal more frequently as My Love's changing behavior became more noteworthy. As I wrote, and then read what I wrote, it became apparent to me that I was living inside my own stories, that old bubble again, and needed an escape hatch!

"Watch for burnout or compassion fatigue! Depression comes after that," someone warned.

How would I know if I burned out? What would indicate depression? I just kept going.

To lighten our otherwise serious lives, we both included snippets of humor in our day-to-day humdrum, which inspired many stories. I needed laughter; I just felt better after happy laughter. Didn't we all? We just needed to allow laughter to come.

My Love had always had a quick wit. He had a knack for what I called "silly segue" humor: picking a word from a sentence someone said in conversation and making a little joke from it.

I'd be talking about a trip I had taken. "While I was in Omaha, they took me to the Strategic Air and Space Museum in Ashland."

"Nothing to see there, eh?"

He'd wait to see if I got it, senseless as it was. He made me laugh, that was enough.

Looking out the window I might comment on what I saw.

"Isn't that the dog-catcher truck parked across the street?"

"They get paid by the pound, you know!"

We embellished any spark of fun, silliness, and amusement for every ounce of laughter we could get. I chuckled while writing and while re-reading, remembering how his eyes used to twinkle when he genuinely laughed. I didn't see that sparkle much anymore.

"What are you laughing about? You're smiling. What is it?" he'd ask me when he saw me become amused as I read the screen in front of me.

Sometimes he would come look at my screen, but mostly he wanted me to tell him. He truly wanted to laugh. We'd laugh together. It felt good to be able to laugh. But it was a bit strange because even when I explained, I realized he seldom understood why I was laughing. He just laughed with me. I knew laughter was healthy, with or without a reason, so we laughed. I wrote stories to help me understand my situations. It helped me sort out what was happening. But also, I hoped potential caregivers might read my stories and feel more confidence in knowing others had made it through unfamiliar circumstances. Plus, they needed to laugh too.

I wondered if all caregivers lived in bubbles filled with anxiety, frustration, pain, suffering, amid times of joy and happiness. It was sometimes nice for me to transport out to find some healing stillness, calm pictures or soft music, even a few encouraging words.

I hoped readers would come to understand caregiving was not a precise science and didn't have to become a career. Just maybe, as it had been for me, caregiving could become a gift, their own discovered buried treasure.

I was grateful to have been able to add caregiving to my life's accomplishments; it had been far more satisfying than I ever anticipated; more rewarding than I could have believed possible. Even though I was reluctant to admit it, I suspected the gift of caregiving was my buried treasure.

7 CONFESSIONS

"I am going to have to learn to be a what?"

How could I forget the day I was designated My Love's caregiver? That was not long after My Love was officially diagnosed with mixed dementia. I say "designated" because it was a position of circumstance and necessity, although eventually, it became a position of choice. I had much to learn about the role.

Who sees caregiving in their future? Not me! I was still young, too busy living life. My background did not include family members caring for one with dementia. Maybe My Love had senility. That's what I thought seniors got. Afterall, he was a young senior in the beginning. And he was only a bit forgetful. I had been ambushed.

I confess, it took time for my resistance to my new role to transform from resentment to acceptance and then to dedicated commitment. I found excuses everywhere I could.

My hippie years taught me to go with the flow, living each moment as it came. Would Eckhart Tolle, who wrote *The Power of Now*, recognize the metamorphosis of his words? Did I still understand?

Probably the most significant change for me was to learn, to actually admit, that nothing was as important as being sure My Love was ok. I became more flexible, laid-back, and I lived in the moment more than ever before! If "it" didn't matter, "it" never reached my priority list! Nothing was worth adding more anxiety into our lives. My Love seemed to have enough apprehension worrying about his own diseases, as evidenced by his anxiety attacks.

In my role as caregiver, one of the main tasks I had was keeping stress out of our lives as much as possible. "Taking a breath and counting to ten" was part of the art of patience I had yet to master. So, as a caregiver I had to learn quickly to back off in my moments of impulsive and impatient responses.

My new responsibility was as much a "doing" role as a "thinking" role. Planning, preparing, anticipating, and scheduling were allocated to the caregiver's wheelhouse, where I learned to navigate through the events and changes we experienced together.

More than that, I was doing and thinking for two. And when my thinking and planning didn't work out as my partner liked, or for any other reason, I was taking the hit, the blame. He didn't have any responsibility because he hadn't thought of it. At times, that part of the role made me resentful. Unjust judgement was indeed unfair, especially from one who couldn't have done nor thought alone.

Being the caregiver, the added responsibilities of "my lady," washer woman, shower coordinator, fashion planner, appointment secretary and entertainment manager, banker, budget manager and bill payer, handyman, education supervisor as well as student, art encourager, taxi driver, navigator, meal planner, waitress, grocery shopper, family vet, pharmacy delivery boy, medicine monitor, and administrator left the sometimes-cook and only-sometimes housekeeper decidedly in last place. And I could never call in sick! You'd have thought I was the mother of helpless young kids.

Activities for me? After a while, I could not even remember what I used to do alone. I didn't know what I'd do even if I had the time. I had given it all up.

I had stopped going for "my" personal services and activities. No haircut, no manicures, and no pedicures. I missed my talks with my dear esthetician of over twenty years. My doctor visits, my library trips, all had to be worked into a schedule where My Love would be in a safe place when not with me. Or he went with me, when he could or would. Those moments in time were not so easy to assign in advance. It was difficult to make arrangements. The number of weeks between appointments increased to months and then years.

I never dreamed the retail online "chat" agent would become my social life, but it happened. I spent time browsing for glasses so "we" could discuss something I thought I'd buy. Then I'd talk to the postman when I sent back my purchase, availing myself of the free returns!

How I wished my dog could talk!

Worst of all, on reflection, I, me, the caregiver, apparently no longer seemed important. I didn't even recognize that the quicksand had taken me.

No more coffee with friends. No music lessons. No art classes. I wasn't putting on make-up in the mornings. No mani-pedi or esthetician dates. Even time for my life-saving therapist became a luxury! I noticed I had t-shirts on inside out, that my socks did not match, and what's more, I did not seem to care. Was I too depressed at that point to realize what had happened? Who would have told me, anyway?

Meaningful conversations with My Love became faint recollections. I noted his vague responses began to replace rational dialogue. Sometimes the topic of a discussion was too painful for me, or difficult for him, to continue because of his inability to find words he wanted to say.

"The trees . . ." he'd say beginning a thought, waving his arms, trying to bring out the words. "Those trees are . . . up there."

Often, he could not find words to explain his beloved canopy of trees that we drove through on a regular basis; he no longer could find his descriptions. He used to tell me about the silhouettes made by dormant oak trees, the shadows their looming trunks left on the street in front of us, but the words were no longer there. Even the drama of the changing colors of fall leaves and the ice-covered branches in winter couldn't revive his lost vocabulary. He'd lose interest when words failed him, and he'd sit silently.

"I had a business that did things. You know . . . for people," he said, trying to explain his complex trade show exhibit business to a new friend. The right words never surfaced. Then his word-finding and periods of clarity declined further.

He would ask me, more than once, "How did the furniture from my parents' home get here?"

He'd glance around in our apartment and point to a table or cabinet "my father made," or a bench he had had as a boy. He never remembered he and I had purchased them for our home twenty-five years earlier. His father's chair, which we did have, probably was the trigger for the entire thinking process.

Don't sweat the small stuff!

And later it was not our apartment, but his apartment, and he wondered what I was doing in it! That's more than losing clarity, I thought.

Dang that dementia!

One night he handed me his phone as he introduced me to his brother. "I want you to meet my new lady!"

He was introducing me as someone new. Phone in hand, I realized it was my turn to talk! His brother learned of his twin's changes mostly during phone "conversations." I knew it must have been hard for him, just as it had been for me.

My Love tried his best, but he had lost his ability to express his thoughts beyond the one or two words of his scripts. Not everyone heard the subtleties because they weren't truly listening. Or they politely never mentioned it.

Eventually, people realized he was no longer able to follow the thread of a conversation. My disappointment came when I realized his smile and nodding head were among his best acting skills, reliving his hard-wired scripts, not conversation-sharing at all. The sadness heightened when I recognized I'd heard those scripts following the many years of serious afternoons spent at the bar.

How long has he had memory loss?

Then the words didn't quite fit the use. He chose words he could find, but they meant nothing in the context of what he was trying to say. His conversations ended up being like an inconsistent code he was trying to use. Babble.

Often, I tended to lose sight of the fact that dementia tended to exhibit a "going backwards" related to learning, a function opposite of what we learned as normal. I have to say, Benjamin Button never acted like this! But I was totally unprepared for any strong emotions or the associated aggressive behaviors related to dementia. It was just more on-the-job learning experience.

I listened to My Love. But for conversation, I talked to other caregivers, neighbors, shopkeepers, what few friends I had left, and family. And mostly to myself.

Me, myself and I spent lots of time together and became well acquainted. Mostly, I talked to myself, a lot.

And then I wrote.

During the middle stages of his dementia, I was socializing far less and writing far more because I could not leave My Love alone.

For some reason he was not nice to others, especially service workers who came to stay with him.

"You are going to have to leave. I have plans," he'd tell them, standing to impose his body in front of them so they'd leave.

Then I'd get a phone call.

"You have to come home. The man has to leave. I have things to do." He would then hang up.

Then I'd get a second phone call, from the service worker.

"He wants me to leave. I told him I can't, but he stands and tells me I must or he will push me out."

I never knew exactly how to settle that conflict from the parking lot of the library or sitting in my car watching the waves, my respite spots. So, I'd go home.

Have I been played as a fool this whole time?

My Love didn't welcome the idea of someone staying with him so that I could go out. I thought he was selfish. I imagine it was more likely he was just scared and selfish. I knew many other caregivers faced similar objections. I just personally could not endure that daily combat. It exhausted me. I could not detach.

As a result, I had to stay home with My Love. I felt I was being punished! It was a somewhat solitary time, even for a loner. I hoped I could recover from the relentless feeling of wanting to give up, of feeling woefully despondent. I never thought such loneliness, such a sense of futility and despair, would happen to me. But for a time, I could not shake off those foggy feelings; the surreal world was winning.

I had been in many social settings, even spoken in front of groups various times over the years. During one Alzheimer Society meeting, I had a comment I wanted to contribute.

I began to speak. "You were talking about . . ."

I lost my train of thought. I truly struggled to get it back, clutching one word, linking it to the next. I worried I had fallen prey to the "use it or lose it" syndrome.

I can't catch dementia, can I?

Having socialized less, had I lost the ability to talk out loud? Was my mind moving faster than my ability to speak? I had noticed in the mirror that my mouth seemed to be physically vanishing. Could all that be true?

From then on, I knew I needed to slow down and keep talking out loud to others. I could not become isolated with My Love, who no longer could hold a conversation with me, who wanted to go nowhere.

Reminders . . . I must talk out loud! We must get out more!

Thank goodness for our special Lifeliner Group caregivers. I could talk with them, say anything to them, have a full conversation. Lifelines were of supreme importance!

~

I used to say, "We never trained to be seniors." But comedian, George Burns said, "By the time you're eighty years old you've learned everything." Of course, he added his punch line, "You only have to remember it."

He was right, of course. In fact, all our lives we had been in training to become a senior! We learned through experiences, through difficult times, through successes and failures, happy moments and sad, unknowingly being strengthened for our golden years, those best years of our lives . . .! Right?

Reflecting, I could see My Love and I had gotten through lots of stressful times in our lives. Businesses, relationships, parents, sports, hobbies, communities all played roles in our lives, each with stresses that contributed to our emotional reactions as aging retirees, the mature ones. Having our own families before we got together added a separate dimension to the story of our stress.

Even before I knew My Love, like most of us, I experienced apprehensions. To me, getting through stress never meant we had left it behind us, it just indicated we had been able to cope with tense and worrying times.

Stress was still around. It played a huge role in my life, creating continual emotional and mental tension. I was always looking for balance, one success, one defeat, one achievement. It seemed I was floundering along forever but surviving.

~

Upon reflection, life seemed to have prepared me for what was ahead. Two examples stood out for me.

When I was in middle school, I loved to run. We lived in the country, on a four-acre hillside, until I was about ten years old. My sister and I climbed up and rolled down that hill. I ran up to the woods and down to the grove of pine trees by the road, following our dog all over the open expanse. I could swing on a monkey-rope tied to a tree branch and then climb that tree, or I could jump that rope, single or Double-Dutch.

After we moved into town, it was nothing for me to walk to see a friend or walk up the road to the small store. At age ten my parents presented me with a bike. I rode back and forth up and down the street where I had permission to be. During middle grades, my friend and I went to the roller-skating rink on the weekends. Two afternoons after school I swam at the YMCA in one of their synchronized groups. My sister and I walked blocks from the mid-city bus stop to church choir practice for weeks. I loved all physical activity. I was healthy, in shape, and energetic for one soon to be a teen, going through puberty.

I especially loved to run. At age twelve, I was running in a school race. Midway down the field, I dropped to the ground. I had not stumbled nor tripped. I just dropped. The weakness came on suddenly. My legs no longer wanted to carry me. I couldn't get up. My legs just had no power, no strength.

What I do remember, even today, was how humiliating it was that I could not finish that race. How embarrassed I felt in front of my classmates that someone had to come on the field to help me get up. I don't recall what words anyone said to me; I just know how I felt. I was disgraced, afraid, confused. Stress.

It was difficult getting back on my feet, even to walk off the field. My mother came to pick me up from school. No one knew exactly what to tell her. The school nurse confirmed a few knee scrapes, but no bones seemed broken. I heard someone say I had thrown the race, dropped to the ground, so I did not have to run. At that time, I had never heard of such a thing. I don't know why they thought that, but I knew it was not true. Even now it makes no sense. I knew I loved to run. It felt very strange not being able to explain and realizing that adults did not believe me, just because they did not understand. That was one of the first experiences when I had been uncomfortable around adults in authority. That was when I learned distrust.

I lived with muscle weakness, no power, for five more years before doctors were able to diagnose me with myasthenia gravis. Very few doctors were familiar with any form of myasthenia gravis in 1960. At that point, it had been researched very little and had no protocol for proper examination.

Perhaps when I was in my fifties, I heard it reported on TV that during the 1950s, it was acceptable among some medical professionals to not completely tell the truth to their patients, a philosophy that supposedly lasted through the turn of the century. I was surprised. Evidently, doctors felt they were kinder by fibbing than if they would have told their patients or the parents, "I don't know what is wrong with her" or, "We don't really know a lot about her condition."

Was it kinder? I had recently been told, in relation to My Love and his ongoing dementia, that I might have to confabulate, tell little white lies, to avoid confusion and confrontation and to keep the peace. Was it kinder? Maybe it was, even though (in my opinion) I felt some doctors were more than unprofessional. I should never have been able to hear their discussions, which I recall vividly sixty-five years later!

While my parents were looking for a diagnosis for my pains, I overheard one physician tell my mother, "Your daughter just wants attention."

Another doctor advised my parents, "It's just growing pains, she'll outgrow it."

"She's sleep-deprived," another doctor diagnosed. "She just needs more sleep."

The doctor who gave me cortisone shots in my knees suggested my knees were inflamed from overactivity.

One specialist was considering that I had a motor neuron disease. We moved before he did anything.

Special shoes made no difference when I was walking.

And the catch-all was, "It's probably a virus. She'll get over it."

Misdiagnosis or missed diagnosis equaled a string of excuses. It did not matter. Nothing helped.

All the while, I was distrusting respected adults more and more each time.

I was a desperate soul, expecting more from the medical community. But since those years I learned that while doctors knew quite a bit, they were learning new information daily! I am grateful I learned the reality of expectations back then.

Years passed. Studies were completed. Articles were published in medical journals. Myasthenia gravis began to get brief mention in neurology class curriculums.

I lived in three states before a neurologist/diagnostician, who was also a professor of neurology at my university, took time for an exhaustive history and a thorough examination so that he could deliver an accurate interpretation of those tests.

After seven years, I was then nineteen, a doctor finally diagnosed my illness during my second year in university. Myasthenia gravis was slow to be understood. Stress caught the blame, as in many diseases where they really didn't know the cause. In the years after I was first diagnosed, studies produced a change in original thought about the physiology and functionality related to MG.

I soon became the guest subject in my doctor's medical neurology class when the topic of myasthenia gravis came up. I was introduced on stage, without the medication I normally took every four hours. The doctor then put me through activities that resulted in typical MG reactions so that his students could observe how the disease presented.

I felt I was the experimental lab rat for those med students who otherwise might never have seen that disease in their practice. It was such an uncomfortable, self-conscious experience, being exposed in front of my student peers. Eventually, I had to switch universities to avoid more years of presentation.

I lived persistence. Gratefully, my past had taught me to keep looking for a correct diagnosis for My Love.

When I fell on that school field, my muscles were giving out; that drop was the first time I felt weak in that way. I lived with chronic myasthenia gravis for over twenty-five years in total, through high school and university years, through two pregnancies, and up through the very day my first marriage ended.

I am quite sure I transformed from an extrovert to an introvert through the years. I saw the world from inside my bubble as the world went spinning around me. I created that bubble for my own protection. It appeared I would later live in that bubble with My Love and his diseases.

In those earlier years, if someone felt awkward being around me because of my reduced physical abilities, I retreated. If people didn't want to talk to me, I stayed in the background. If I anticipated fear, I left. My bubble was a safe place. I learned social behavior by watching, vicariously interacting, from within my bubble. It was a real place, even if only in my mind.

I knew it sounded strange to say, but I was very fortunate. Twenty-six years after the day I fell in that eighth-grade race, about age thirty-nine, myasthenia gravis began to go into a state of remission. I was told that was because I had had a thymectomy in the year of diagnosis. Or maybe the stars just aligned for me!

After that, myasthenia was nearly non-existent in my life. However, when I became really tired, exhausted, I secretly worried that stress as a caregiver might awaken myasthenia and make it return, full steam. But what could I do? I still had to live.

I directed my intention to overcome my physical and mental obstacles throughout my life. I kept my mental responses positive. But I turned inward to keep my focus from distraction. I didn't look in the mirror too much, seldom wore make-up. For years, I colored my hair, I think to hide who I really was. I thought a lot. I saw and took in events and emotions that others lived. I wrote about them as if I were experiencing them myself. As always, my therapy, my outlet, was putting my reactions into words.

I could do little about my physical situation. I accepted it. I focused on dealing with what I could and could not do anymore. I was drawn to positive energy. Or was it drawn to me? It was no surprise that in later years I was attracted to reiki, energy medicine, and therapeutic touch. I liked the feeling of good energy surrounding me.

I looked back on those twenty-five years of illness, and knew those experiences provided knowledge and strength that helped me fight through more recent stress. I took on challenges and built up my confidence despite myasthenia gravis, or, just maybe, because of it.

And here I was, going through similar stresses again, but with My Love.

~

Another very stressful situation came much later in life when I was boating with My Love. We were a mile off the north shore of the lake, just west of the city.

While we were casually cruising home from a weekend on nearby islands with friends, the steering locked up on My Love's forty-foot powerboat. We weren't going fast, but a powerboat generally moves swiftly on the water, even at a slow speed. For some reason, the rudder was stuck in a position where we could only go in circles.

My Love pulled back on the throttles. There we sat in the bouncy water and idled, drifting in circles, going nowhere. The steering cable would not allow the rudder to straighten so that the boat could move forward. A strong wind was coming up. Round and around we went.

Next, I heard, "You'll have to take the wheel, while I go below to see if I can fix the problem."

I had steered *Love Boat* in calm waters many times, but never in such choppy waves. For sure, I had never navigated on just a wing and a prayer.

What happens if we don't get into a harbor before rough waters reach us?

My Love was puttering around below.

He yelled up to me, "I don't have the right tools." I heard some swear words mixed in there somehow, but then his voice faded away.

Alone, up on the bridge, I could not move. I felt my body begin to freeze up. I was terrified.

Powerful waves were building. The approaching winds began to pitch *Love Boat* up and down. Other boats passed us, not less than ten meters away.

I watched as they left us in their wake, speeding toward a nearby marina. Their passengers waved. No one realized we were in trouble, even with our engines idling, bouncing in the water. Because of the winds, I was not sure you could tell that we were just idling, but I became frightened that no one was going to stop to help us.

Boats had accidents all the time. I did not want to be remembered only by front page headlines, "Two Lost on Lake in Wake of Storm."

The wind picked up. As I sat topside at the wheel, alone and unsure what to do, I sensed My Love was below for a very long time.

Finally, he yelled up to me, "Try to call for help. You are going to have to use the radio to make a Mayday call." Again, he disappeared below.

Life and property were at risk and assistance was essential. We had a real emergency.

My Love had never taught me to use the ship-to-shore VHF radio on board. I had seen and heard other captains use it. I had heard other calls come across through the speakers. Now My Love wanted me to make a call.

I can still feel how terrified my body felt, the fear going through my shaking hands as I held the VHF speaker, all alone on the bridge of a six-ton boat in strong winds! I was operating on autopilot! The stress was intense. I did not know what was going to happen to the boat next and it was going to be up to me to get someone to help us.

I pushed the distress button. "Mayday. Mayday. Mayday," I heard myself saying. Someone came back and suggested I change the frequency. Luckily, I knew how to do that. Then I repeated my call. "Mayday. Mayday. Mayday. This is *Love Boat. Love Boat. Love Boat.* Mayday. Mayday. Mayday. Over."

I waited. I heard crackling.

Then I heard someone return the call. "*Love Boat*, is that you?" they asked, using the name of the boat. I recognized the caller's voice.

"*Love Boat*, what is the nature of your emergency? Do you need help?" Someone was listening!

I did not know the proper protocol. What was I supposed to say? I was glad I knew the person talking to me. I had no idea of our specific location. Luckily, we were near shore and I could identify buildings. Whoever was on the VHF would have to ask me questions.

Damn, where is our GPS?

We again changed channels to talk.

"Yes, *Love Boat*'s steering went out. The rudders are not in a straight position. We don't seem to be able to go straight, and My Love can't reconnect the steering. We can't get into port. What should I do?" I shouted everything I knew in one breath.

Other captains overheard our conversation. Two boats showed up to help us get to safety before strong winds made it impossible. As each of the boats bounced higher and lower in the waves, I was at a loss to find the strength to keep our rescue boat's bowsprit from hitting us broadside, even with the aid of our boat hook pole. Her captain's competence was amazing!

On that day, it took me several tries to catch a line, but once I was able to grab hold, I held tight while fastening it to a cleat. After all my excitement, My Love arrived back on the bridge in time to hold the wheel as we were towed toward shelter.

Deep breath.

Once in safe harbor, My Love found someone to help figure out the steering. Thankful.

That fear, that intense stress, interrupted my intention to make the Mayday call in the first place. Ironically, I was forced to confront my fears to be able to make my call. The conflict and the trauma that I felt while we were floating chipped away at my confidence. But somehow, by finding my courage, I made the call, and we avoided an ending I wouldn't want to consider.

These two extremely memorable events, surrounded by anxiety, caused me serious stress at the time. I was grateful to have made it through the fears associated with both. What I learned became part of my "revised DNA," the newer, stronger, less fearful, hopefully, more resistant to stress, calmer me.

I believe it was overcoming those fears that gave me the strength and wisdom to recognize that I would be strong enough to be a caregiver. I was not trained, but I evolved. I found a way to do what had to be done, thankfully with lots of help, as we all must eventually do.

And that is what I came to understand caregivers had to do. I had to confess that, conditioned or not, we had to find ways to get beyond the stress, to go on with life. All the support just made that an easier task. I never stopped asking questions. I continued being persistent. I knew no other way.

~

After I finished writing about our day drifting in circles, I read the story to My Love. I wanted to see if he remembered anything about that dreadful day out on the lake well over twenty years earlier, how afraid we had been. Even though he shook his head yes, I could tell he really could not recall the event.

Repeating my words, he told me, "Maybe. It happened out on the lake." That was the best he could do.

Sadly, he could not add any specifics to my story. He could not tell me who had rescued us, what had happened to the steering, who fixed the boat, or even how he felt at the time. But then, those were details that even I did not remember!

I had tried to rescue that memory for him, but I think the memory was too terrifying, or I was too late. He heard my story as a story.

"Hunh!" he said, as if to tell me "that's an interesting story," and turned away.

He did not connect with it. His memory of that event was, indeed, gone.

Again, I was the one who was sad.

He didn't even know he had forgotten.

8   MEET MY LOVE

"I was never sick. Why would I ever go to a doctor?" My Love explained when I asked why he had no doctor.

I quit asking him sometime after five years.

Even when we got together twenty-plus years earlier, he remembered having no family doctor. He boasted that because he was seldom sick, he did not need a doctor. He was pleased with how fit and healthy he was. Granted, he kept a fit appearance when he was quite active. He loved to joke with me and say he had "the body of a Greek god!" Twenty years earlier, yes, he had had a more physically tuned body! *Didn't we all?*

He'd been a skiing instructor for a few years. He had been a lifeguard at the beach. He had climbed around on his boats, on the water and when docked. He had been active installing exhibits his company built. He still loved to walk. His body needed to move and had stayed in physical shape as a result. Some of those years were still in his long-term memory bank.

Even in his seventies, his body, while smaller, still carried him effortlessly when he walked thirty blocks a day. But as he moved through his seventies, disease changed his life.

Nevertheless, during his more than three-quarters-of-a-century life, he had seen very few doctors, and when he had, they met in an emergency room.

During a fall on a ski slope in his early thirties, he splintered his tibia, that long shinbone that connects the knee to the ankle. He still had a six-inch scar across that knee. It was just about the only story he could tell when doctors took a medical history!

My Love explained, "A tree got in my way, and I hit it." He admitted he felt rather faint when he saw his bone coming through the snow. "It was then I realized it was my bone that was protruding through my skin, sticking straight out," he finished, always reaching way out to show me how far out his bone was. Just like the fishermen, he always bragged, "It was th-i-s-s-s big!"

The ski patrol took him to paramedics and nurses and eventually he was transported to a hospital for medical attention. Adding to his story, he insisted, "I wore a cast for some time, but I wasn't sick."

Another time, in his fifties, My Love quickly jumped off his boat onto the dock and caught his thigh on an exposed, jagged, metal edge of a top-side safety stanchion bar. That was basically a pipe without a protective end cover. That long, deep gash required stitches. His calm reaction and lack of emotion revealed his high threshold for pain! It made me wonder if he had that same high level of resistance to accepting his current illnesses. He just did not accept his diagnosis.

In general, he did appear to have lived a healthy life. He was right; he rarely had had even a sneeze since I met him.

He bragged to me, "Even when they took out my appendix, I wasn't sick. Who needs a doctor if you're not sick?"

I always felt his dismissive comment was rather reminiscent of words in the old-time song "The Arkansas Traveler," telling me his cabin isn't leaking when it's not raining.

There was no way My Love could anticipate the changes that would take place when diseases took hold of his body. He never saw the transformations coming! Had he fallen into head-in-the-sand thinking? Or worse, was he relying on out-of-sight, out-of-mind justification?

My Love retired at age sixty-nine. Initially, I saw no significant changes, physical or mental, from day to day. He still went to meet his drinking buddies in the afternoon. He still went to his boat or the boat club on weekends. Of course, he was home much more, and we were together much more, but he seemed the same person he was before retirement. I guess we needed separation for me to see the changes.

But looking back since his retirement, putting some space between then and now, I could compare how he changed; and those changes were significant. Forgetful moments which I had attributed to senility were happening far too often. But because I saw him every day, I missed many signs until I started journaling.

Mostly, when he could, he wanted to be active with his drinking cronies at his boat. Taking in the sun, talking, playing in the water, and, yes, going for boat rides. He had lived and breathed in the boating world for over sixty years, owning various styles of boats. And then the hardest day of his life came. He could no longer physically handle his forty-foot, six-ton powerboat and had to sell it. He had no replacement pastime, no alternative hobby to fill that vacuum. Life kept changing, dramatically.

My Love still needed friends. He had always loved being with people, and as part of that sense of socialness, he loved looking nice.

Wearing what he loved had been a distinguishing expression of his personality for as long as I had known him! Considered a nice dresser, he liked wearing nice clothes: pressed pants, even his jeans, shirts that had to be dry cleaned (I did not iron much anymore!) instead of t-shirts, and shined leather shoes, no runners, and, rarely now, boat shoes. He cared that his hair was combed and parted properly and trimmed in a certain way. Tidy, neat, clean, and fashionable. Everything was in place.

Since his diagnosis, he still had tendencies toward socialness and fashion, just much less. His standard dress became khaki pants, plaid shirt and suede slippers that looked like shoes, but fit his swollen feet.

Age, along with the yet-unknown reduced oxygen in My Love's lungs, must have slowed his actions, and reduced his strength. The onset of mild cognitive impairment, the precursor to his oncoming Alzheimer's disease, revealed itself slowly, affecting his thinking skills, causing forgetful incidents we laughingly called "senior moments." We had no reference points for Alzheimer's disease with family or friends. Permanent memory loss had never crossed our minds.

As time went on, I knew My Love's memory loss was more than senior absentmindedness. I was tuned-in to his random, inconsistent daily shifts. Flexibility, mine, became a keyword.

I began to realize that I could not make sense of his world and that My Love could not teach me. I was floundering on my own.

My Love had been diagnosed first with Chronic Obstructive Pulmonary Disease, COPD. I had to learn what those intimidating words meant, what adjustments we needed to make in our home to accommodate any changes ahead. Air cleaners, humidifier, dehumidifier, medications, inhalers, puffers, diet changes, and activity schedules were added to our inventory for maintenance, along with our once-simple dusting and vacuuming routine.

My priority was to keep a balance between each of our needs as much as possible. After all, I was aging right along with My Love. It took time even to understand what my new tasks and goals would be and to evaluate if I would be able to keep up, which was not always guaranteed.

Fortunately, from the beginning, My Love did not experience coughing spells that pro-duced phlegm. He did not suffer incapacitating asthma attacks. Originally, he walked thirty blocks every day with the dog to help his body fend off those conditions.

In those early days, I thought he was fortunate not to have the severe level of COPD that I had read about. Respirologists could see areas of his lungs where emphysema was closing in, but generally his lungs were declared clear.

I was grateful his doctor was able to discover that My Love had dementia. I understood that at first My Love took written tests that focused on memory, counting, reasoning, and language skills. With those results, the doctor was able to make his diagnosis by adding a neurological evaluation, My Love's medical history, and results from lab tests, x-rays, CT scans, and an MRI.

I was always surprised that his GP had tested for memory loss in the first place. I wondered what warning signs My Love's doctor noticed that I ignored. I was quite sure My Love would never have considered asking about his memory.

But his doctor assured me as he scrolled through his notes from earlier in their association that My Love had not been able to discuss his simple medication schedule clearly, which had prompted the doctor's suspicions. My Love paid no attention to his illnesses. His smart young doctor did his job. Thank goodness he followed up with testing.

The advanced science and technology known for Alzheimer's disease amazed me. I learned how scans picked up precise areas in My Love's brain, showing where the plaques and tangles were actively causing trouble. The technology saw where My Love had had small strokes, causing vascular dementia.

Did My Love forget names of his long-time friends? And then later close family members and then, even me? Yes, yes, and yes. How did I miss signs that were right in front of me? There were times I was surprised when I observed changes in his attitude. Was that memory loss or old age? His or mine? Or something else?

Did he fade in and out of conversations? He did, but I thought it was senioritis, or more a lack of interest. At first, when he would answer "Yeh!" or "I know!" or "Right!" or even chuckle a bit, I believed he was staying with the conversation.

Alas, often he never had been "with it" in the first place. Perhaps I should have recognized memory loss when he used those canned and scripted responses too often. I didn't.

~

Despite everything, he was an old retired guy. And after retirement, we were together too much, I was not paying enough attention to him. I wondered if he was becoming bored at times, like when he played his iPad solitaire for hours.

Now he is an old retired guy with no hobby.

He needed a hobby, a diversion. Nothing interested him.

Did I miss the signs when he repeated questions that I had already answered?

"Was it busy over there?" he'd ask when I went out, anywhere.

"Yes, a lot of people were on the road." I might answer. "It's a long weekend. People are shopping for family parties."

I wouldn't have time to count to sixty before he'd ask again. "Was it busy today?" Or, "How many people were out there today?" Funny, he sometimes did put a little spin on it. But I'm sure he did not remember asking before.

"Yes," I would answer after the third or fourth time I heard a similar question, one right after the other. I gave up making a conversation and instead just calmly replied.

Initially, I was not alerted to memory loss by repeated questions; I thought he just wasn't listening to my answers. He asked the same questions multiple times. I answered every time. It did no good to get upset or to call him out on it. He didn't realize he was asking the same questions. He couldn't change that behavior now.

Even after he lost his cell phone and My Love had no idea where to look for it, I was slow to realize the association with his progressing memory loss. He seldom lost anything. I just thought it was one of those things. The odds. We never found the phone.

Although still learning about memory loss, I began thinking his loss of focus and his anger and anxiety were all associated with his new diseases. What else would be that dramatic?

Thankfully, My Love's doctor was quick to tune in to his new senior patient. They saw each other often in the beginning. My Love was making up for his years not having a family doctor. He went alone to appointments in those first years.

So, once COPD and dementia diseases had been diagnosed and medications seemed under control, the ongoing pain in My Love's chest became the target of our probes. His pain was located at the crossroads of his torso, the roundhouse through which all systems seemed to pass, especially nerves. Even his young doctor was having trouble pin-pointing the elusive cause, since he never saw the mystery incident, what My Love and I began calling an episode.

I tried to video an episode on my phone, so I could show his doctor. The video seldom represented what I saw with my eyes. I couldn't pull the various sections together to make sense.

We kept asking doctors at the walk-in clinic and the emergency room, but no one could identify the cause of his pain with certainty. The coughing and breathlessness that made up his episodes seemed to have no physical medical explanation.

I asked his doctor, "How can My Love have a pain in his chest, the very same pain, in the very same place, causing the very same symptoms, for over two years and it not be caused by something physical?"

The doctor shook his head. He had been unable to determine what it was except that, like the doctor before him at the clinic, he suggested it was anxiety.

Having never seen anyone else with anxiety, I searched YouTube. Nothing resembled what I was watching day in, day out. There were many to see; they took me hours to watch, but I saw nothing that made me feel better about My Love's attacks. I remained My Love's doctor's number one skeptic for months.

My Love did not have that pain in his chest all the time. Sometimes I asked him about his discomfort.

He'd say, in his Alzheimer's truth, "I haven't had any pain in a long time."

At that moment, he remembered no pain. At other times he might seem to recall the pain but knew he did not have any pain right then. But, in a rare no-memory-loss moment, he would be lucid and could tell me all about it, as if he were aware while having the episode. Damned dementia!

Like his Alzheimer's disease, the chest pain seemed to come and go, but his episodes seemed to appear on a schedule. I learned that the anxiety and coughing that began around 4 p.m. were likely part of sundowning, a time of increased confusion and restlessness. Associated with the middle stages of Alzheimer's disease, those behaviors seemed to occur at that later sundown time of day.

I never heard a description given for the episodes he began having in the mornings. Maybe I should have experimented with marijuana oil in his meals for intervention of at least one of his diseases!

First, they told us his chest pain was phlegm, caught in his airway, that could not be released. Some doctors admitted they could not be sure if his pain were caused by phlegm or not, especially since he rarely showed any signs of mucus or phlegm at regular times.

Then, anxiety was suggested. Maybe it was anxiety, but I kept waiting for something visible to show up. I could feel an anxiety, but I couldn't see an anxiety. I trudged on, keeping my mind open to other ideas for a disease with physical symptoms.

It took over five years to discover a correct diagnosis of my disease, myasthenia gravis, in the 1950s and '60s. We could yet find an answer for My Love's chest pain. I could not give up. I wouldn't give up.

Early gastroscopies indicated nothing in My Love's mid-chest location. Personally, my layperson thinking told me that any pain from breathing had to do with his lungs. Doctors cautiously said no, because scans and x-rays showed nothing in that area. But My Love always said it felt like he couldn't breathe, even though he could. My obvious rationale said breath-related meant lung-related.

One of my doctors, who had never met My Love but knew my story, asked me if I really wanted to pursue it anymore, did I truly want to know? I think he realized my frustrations were getting in my way of clear thinking for the other things in my life.

I thought on that a lot! Why did my sometimes-coroner doctor ask it like that? What did he suspect? I wondered if my doctor knew something I didn't want to know. Or did he want me to be sure I was thinking about myself? He was also my therapist, after all. Was he speaking honestly about his concern for me and my ability to continue caregiving as well as to carry on my own life? Maybe both.

My Love's mystery disease took up hours of our time trying to discover the cause. It made a huge difference in the plans we made, how we spent our time, where we went, how long we could do things, attention span limitations, foods he ate, and where I went alone and for how long. I could not begin to count the times, over a period of two years, we had gone to doctors and the emergency department when the episodes happened, still I was the only one to witness it! We always came home without an answer. Many, many times.

Scientists explained that stress was a normal part of our life. I had heard some studies showed it served a useful purpose. But stress interfered with My Love's life. His anxiety seemed unhealthy. I was sure he had been literally worrying himself sick for a long time.

In my opinion, My Love had experienced an overload of stress within a five-year period, episodes that might be called traumatic by some. He had been sued into personal bankruptcy, had lost his business of thirty-four years, had separated from his wife of over twenty years, then moved into my apartment. Finally, he retired at sixty-nine and gave up smoking packs of cigarettes a day after nearly fifty years. Not long thereafter, he had to give up his boating life of sixty years. Shortly after his COPD diagnosis, he gave up his beer. Something had to give.

Even I saw a foundation for some level of illness. I did not know what role My Love's stress played, but I felt sure it provided fertile ground for disease to germinate.

Without breathing, obviously, there was no life. I worried about him, his breathing episodes, and his shifting memory situations all the time, whether I was with him or away from him.

One afternoon, when his illnesses seemed to be stable, My Love brought me his cell phone to see. He showed me a photograph of the two of us taken at a dance years before. We were laughing and having fun. Then, without a word, he scrolled to the next screen, a coloring book page that said, "Never Give Up." Finally, he smiled as he scrolled through to one more screen and revealed a picture of a wreath of flowers, with the words "Life is Great!" written in the middle.

I felt like the luckiest caregiver ever.

I knew then that I had been giving care to the person I knew beyond his diseases.

~

It is important to note that during that first two-week hospital stay, when doctors discovered high calcium and kidney issues, a source cause eluded them. Because of medication changes, My Love's dementia progression increased substantially, and his new mystery diseases became leg and knee pains, and separately, groin and abdomen pains.

However, after his first two-week stay in the hospital, for three months My Love rarely had an anxiety attack. Plus, evidence of COPD seemed to disappear. No one knew why. More mystery.

He was using a walker within six weeks of leaving the hospital, where before admission he had been walking thirty blocks a day. Walking to the elevator in our apartment became painful. I felt like I was caring for a different person, with a new set of symptoms. I had to learn all over again how to deal with his issues. Aches and pains, but no anxiety attacks. We both were confused by it all. But we managed.

Three months later My Love was back in the hospital for a second stay, again with high calcium. Once the doctors stabilized the calcium, his pains subsided. He folded up his walker. After eleven different tests, the high calcium was named the likely cause of the muscle aches and groin pains. But we went home a second time without knowing the cause of the calcium spike. Once home, his anxiety and COPD signs returned.

I was totally exhausted.

9   BORN A PAINTER

"Did you study art?" A visitor in our class was speaking to My Love.

When someone walked into our Alzheimer Society creative class, they noticed right away how intent My Love was on his work, how focused he was. The rest of us were enjoying the moment and each other, while his passion for creating with artistic media took him into the zone. I'd just sit waiting to see what would emerge each week. I loved it.

Was My Love born an artist? A painter? I only learned of his earlier painting endeavors years after we retired. I always sensed that his love for art and painting was the connection that drew us together more than halfway through our lives. Was it also the reason he had been associated with designing and building exhibits, the artsy side of industry?

I could tell My Love liked art. Early on, when we would walk by a store with paintings in the window, or through a small gallery, he would slow down his stride and linger. Sometimes I'd catch myself pulling his hand back when he didn't notice the large No Touching sign! Ever the kid!

Usually, I would hear, "Hmmm. Look at that." He'd study the pieces and then move on. He continually showed enough curiosity that I parked that thought in my brain. Yet, we never really talked about his interest as anything he wanted to pursue as a hobby. He was preoccupied with his business and with his true first love, boating.

He had been building up his own exhibit/design company for sixteen years by the time we met.

"Is that why you stayed with it?" I asked him one time after we retired. "You enjoyed hammering and drilling?"

"I guess I liked all the aspects. I liked to build, yes. I liked to silkscreen, back when we did that. I liked the atmosphere."

I could see the sparkle in his eyes come as he spoke of it. I always thought he had a good eye for color and design. He had a steady hand to apply graphics, even in the years before he retired.

"I enjoyed designing, and when I began learning to use the computer, it was just fun."

Computers only came into use in his small business in the later years. Before that, design was done with paper, pencils, drafting scales, compasses, and straight edges, while seated at a drafting table surrounded by good natural lighting. From the beginning, his company had professional exhibit designers who were adept at the drawing-on-paper techniques. The newer designers brought their computer skills and changed how designs were created, and thus, presented.

My Love was absorbed in his exhibit company for over thirty-four years before his luck changed, his life changed, and nothing was as before.

He told me about the early years, about when he and one or two others were the company. As needed, they became the salesmen, the decision makers, the carpenters, and painters. They could all install and drive vans and trucks. Probably they swept floors, as well. They did what had to be done to make the clock move and the money come in. Each one took their turn at what they could do.

But somehow, My Love always ended up in the paint shop. His talents put him in the slot to be the painter when the jobs required. He had the steady hand. He had the eye to mix color. He was the one called upon to check that color output was right. He was a strong one, able to lift the panels or structures into the spray booth. He was the one who never wore a mask.

My Love was one to get things done. He wanted to move on to the next phase, to go back and put on his carpenter's apron to build more parts. That's how the business was in the beginning.

While My Love held the spray gun, his nose was close to the panels, possibly taking in paint spray, as his head turned to check that the color touched evenly upon the surface. He was the one breathing the fumes into his lungs every minute while spraying in the paint area.

The paint spray not only landed on the panel surface where he directed the gun but also on the wall of the paint booth and the floor. Overspray landed in his hair, on his hands, on his overalls. The fumes lingered along with the smell of solvents that he used to remove paint from his hands and face. Even if he were not a born painter, paint was getting under his skin during those years! Over and over, those vapors and chemicals somehow ended up going through his lungs.

However, I believed My Love was a born painter, with a bit more artistic bent than a panel painter. I held to this belief because I watched his passion bloom, maybe resurface in a new way. When we participated in our Alzheimer Society's express and create class, I watched him appreciate the beauty in a setting sun, notice the sparkling ice on tree branches, admire the graceful overhanging trees along the boulevard, or describe the colors in a stormy sky. I watched him paint trees, rivers and skies, and more trees.

In his early retirement years, after the business was gone, My Love spent hours working and playing around his boat. Boating had long been his first love. There was no art, no painting.

Oops, with one exception! He did spray his forty-foot boat bottom annually to reduce marine growth on the water-covered area of the boat, which, he told me, allowed the boat to perform better.

Every year My Love sanded off the peeling paint layers from the bottom, sending chemically filled dust into the air surrounding him. He always prepared the surface suitable for new paint. Still, he worked without a mask.

In the spring he would put one or two coats of blue anti-fouling paint on the bottom and halfway up the sides to the chines. He lay on his back while spraying the toxic biocide. The overspray from several coats floated back down onto his face, into his hair and eyes, onto his clothes. And into his lungs. Still, he seldom wore a mask until later years. Did it make a difference? Who knows?

My Love was meant to be outdoors, in the sun, playing in the water, washing his boat. He chose his boating life, I feel sure, partly because of the associated social life. In those days, I imagine the thought of going off to paint rivers and trees on canvas never crossed his mind.

And then the diagnosis of COPD hit him hard. His doctor told him his lungs could no longer fight the battle. His body was responding to the activities of his younger years. He had not protected his lungs. His years of smoking thousands of heavy cigarettes, his hours of painting in the spray booth and the years he spent under his boat, all without a paint suit or mask protection, now were taking their toll.

My Love's body was rebelling. It was too late. His lungs were reacting to the abuse. Whatever the cause, by the time his test results landed on his doctor's desk, the reports said he was well into the disease. He primarily displayed the emphysema component of the COPD triad, which included chronic bronchitis, and asthma, all with the characteristic of airflow obstruction.

My Love's nagging cough lingered. His cough had only a few of the outlined symptoms, and it never was as severe as I expected for one with COPD. It was sporadic. But later, his coughing flare-ups associated with anxiety, his episodes, could go on for hours.

Then one day he admitted to me that he should have worn a mask every time he used any spray gun;

he acknowledged he should have stopped smoking years sooner. But he knew it was too late. Such a woefully painful moment of realization.

About four years later after his admission, he was diagnosed with mixed dementia. Throughout the learning curve of his diseases, we were in close contact with our local office at the Alzheimer Society. It was through that group that My Love and I found the most appropriate class. They offered a creative class to both caregivers and loved ones.

That class was perfect for folks who sought a creative outlet without any requirement for skill or talent. I missed my years of teaching art. I was excited at the prospect of being in an art class. I was eager for us to be in an art class together.

I asked My Love, "Would you like to be in a program, a weekly class, where you could work with paints and clay and chalks and pencils and scissors. Maybe we both could use watercolor?"

I was struggling to perform a super sell job! I didn't know what to say to him so that he would be as excited as I was, so we could both be in a creative class!

But his response came quickly. "When does it begin?" He was anxious to be part of it, too.

The express and create class brought My Love's story full circle; he was back in a place where he could paint, but where he did not need a mask.

In the class, there were watercolors, acrylic paints, pastels, and chalks to use. Baskets of colored pencils, regular pencils, yarns, glue, sticks, ribbons, and glitter were on the shelf in the cupboard. On the shelves, My Love found paper with lines, without lines, thick, thin, colored, black or white, textured or smooth.

Nearly every week he painted. Regardless of the suggested project for the day, My Love found his way to complete his project by painting. It did not matter that he painted. It mattered that he had a good experience. A positive experience in a social setting.

My Love and I were privileged to participate in that class for over four years. In our living room, we started a gallery wall with his paintings. His theme, unconsciously, was trees and a river. Sometimes he added a boat. Sometimes he put in a building, a house, or birds, animals. But a body of water or a river and trees typically were the subject of the scene, recalling his younger years, perhaps.

The picture frames didn't all match, but they set off his paintings and looked lovely on our wall. Framing them so he could see them on the wall made him feel good. I truly hoped displaying them would encourage him to do more. But too soon, he forgot he painted them.

"I painted those? No!" he'd say, or something similar. "I didn't paint those," he'd repeat, especially when I brought them up a couple years after they'd been on the wall. And then he'd just walk away.

During one class we decorated clear plastic Christmas tree bulbs, putting paint, glitter, pipe cleaners, and decorations on the inside, and from the outside they were lovely. We brought them home. I showed them to him in the evening. He had forgotten already that we had made them. But he had been totally absorbed in the project, now loving the results from our activity earlier that same day.

He worked hard on his paintings. His focus on detail was intense. He knew what he wanted to paint when he started out. And when his work was finished, he knew it was complete, regardless of time allotted.

Without fail, after every class, he said to me, "That is such a good class, don't you think? They sure come up with great projects to do!"

I could only agree, over and over and over, as he repeated it every week during the drive home. That class was the perfect match for a caregiver and a loved one who loved art, especially ideal for the two of us.

There was no doubt My Love was a painter. I thought his joy might be in the process as much as the result. Was he born a painter? It seemed he was, when he was no longer a boater.

10 IT'S ABOUT WE

Thank you, Neil Diamond. "We." Love is all about *we*!

I finally came to understand that. Of course, if My Love were not in my life, there would be no we, no caregiving to admit to, nor to reflect upon. But My Love was in my life and he was the one I journaled about, the one whose stories I shared. He.

Through my writing, I confessed, divulged, talked, and recounted much about my own experiences related to my role as caregiver. That would be about Me.

He. Me. We.

"We" was the perfect song from Neil Diamond, a singer of and from my era. Years before I met My Love, I swayed back and forth while singing along to "Beautiful Noise" and "Brother Love's Travelling Salvation Show." I still loved Neil Diamond's sound and his words, his clear, musical, lyrical, rhythmic, believable words and sound of love! I could hear the words, the music, even years later.

And so, when I heard the familiar sound of "Sweet Caroline" drifting out from the stereo speakers on the bridge of My Love's boat, I was excited to discover he liked Neil Diamond, too! For me, music was magical; it could weld a strong bond between people.

When I played music these days, Neil Diamond as well as other long-time favorites, it somehow stimulated My Love's facial expression. Like in the documentary *Alive Inside*, where music was explored and demonstrated as therapy for those with memory loss, My Love's favorite music seemed to awaken and reboot his accumulation of memories from his earlier years.

His love for easy-listening music was revealed by the smile on his face and twinkle in his eyes, not seen often anymore. An easy-listening piano CD would calm his anxious moments. I noted music often became a successful intervention, similar to what I would soon learn art could be. I just had to remember to turn on the tunes!

Listening to The Eagles, Neil Diamond, Nana Mouskouri, Julio Iglesias, or John Barry movie themes, My Love sometimes got up, and, with a slight bounce to his step, even with pain in his knees, he slid across the room instead of just walking. Maybe it was a senior-shuffle, but I saw a dance step.

"Ahhh! Now that's nice," he'd say approvingly. Then a smile settled on his face.

Once in a while I played some big band music featuring Peter Appleyard, the vibraphone artist. My Love loved the rhythm of the big bands. He would dance and dance.

"I like that music," I'd hear, and again he'd smile and then he'd ask, "who is it?"

I could not tell if he remembered the names, or just asked out of habit.

If a fast jitterbug or a big-band waltz were playing on our oldies radio station, he would grab me and twirl me once and move on. And then he couldn't even do that anymore. But the music still brought a smile.

I had seen music make My Love come alive inside, just like that movie said. He loved to dance when he was just a few years younger; it was obvious how much the music moved him. The growing demand on music and art to take the pains away was exceeding what they seemed to be able to do in his earlier years.

He used to play the spoons—a set of wooden spoons or stainless spoons from the kitchen, tweaked to become musical spoons. I tried getting him to play them again. But he just took the spoons and put them aside. I wasn't sure if he forgot how to play them or just didn't want to play them anymore. Often, he just needed people to energize him, I alone was never enough. Knowing how he loved music, I had to make sure people and music were in his life more often.

Originally, our life had focused a lot on he and me but eventually, our attention was on *we*.

11 ANOTHER BEATING HEART

A pet can be an enjoyable addition to a family. In our case, Mypsy changed My Love's life!

She came to us . . . well, really, we went to find "our dog" and brought home the cutest little Maltese-Poodle-mix puppy. She was such a little princess; fine wavy apricot silk fur with pink skin showing through, dark black, beady eyes, and as much energy, we later discovered, as all the puppies we'd left behind, combined. At eight weeks old, we named her Miss Gypsy. Over the years she became Mypsy.

At first, My Love did not like the idea of a pet, not a dog, not a cat.

"Don't you know if we get a dog we can't go anywhere. We'll be forever cleaning up after a pet. Someone has to feed a dog and walk it." He was adamant and had no plans to be the walker or the feeder. He wanted me to feel the same way. But I liked the idea of a walking companion.

He tried to convince me it was a mistake. "I can't believe you have even considered a dog!" he scolded me, thinking he'd settled it as he walked away from me. I was surprised because I'd been told how much he loved his dogs in earlier years. And then, somehow, unprompted, he turned to me and said, in a total reverse of attitude, "Ok." He agreed to it. That was it. I was elated.

After My Love had been diagnosed with COPD, but before we had any thoughts of dementia, I had an inner nagging to get a dog. I wanted a dog. The vet assured me that the breed we had chosen would not likely shed, and thus not be a problem for someone with COPD. He'd had dogs in his younger years, so, with any luck, he would not be allergic to pet dander. Probably, such a puppy would be able to stay with us.

Animals have always completed a family picture for me. Another beating heart, a giver of love (I never bought into that unconditional love part!), a friendly face anytime one is needed! Someone to converse with without talking to myself! I was talking about a dog! A dog whose excitement to see me open my eyes made me glad to hear the alarm in the morning. A dog whose presence filled the room with happiness. My dogs always had such sweet personalities. I missed that beautiful feeling of contentment while cuddling with a puppy or grown family pet. Expectations!

My Love agreed to go with me to bring home the puppy I had chosen from puppies available nearby. We spent the hottest day of the year that July driving two hours to get our little dog. My Love grumbled the entire time, about the heat, about the distance, about the traffic, about the time it took to go such a distance in the heat, just for a dog.

When we saw our tiny apricot furball, she was exactly like her photograph. She was obviously the runt, half the size of her smooth, peachy colored sister and frizzy, white brothers. She was curled in the back corner of the pen. Although her sister was adorable, our puppy still was the one I wanted, even after seeing all six in her litter running around together.

I picked her up. She fit comfortably in the palm of my hand.

My chosen little girl did not move much. Oh, good! A quiet little thing! I passed her to My Love. She snuggled right down onto his chest. He did not expect that!

The owner quietly mentioned to My Love, "That puppy will probably pick you as master, just watching how she is reacting to you right now."

Sales pitch? It did not matter. She was adorable. I knew she would love us both, as most dogs would.

Coming home, she cried, and My Love could not keep her from scratching him. So, we traded places; he gave her to me to hold while he drove.

Our puppy did cry. She scratched. But she settled down and slept the entire way home cuddled to my chest. She had worn herself out.

When we knew we were getting a dog, we purchased a kennel for a full-grown medium-sized dog. Our puppy did not even reach the first wire when she stood on her back feet, but she was just big enough so that she couldn't fit through the openings on the sides. There were five wires to the top. She would grow in time, just never much past the second wire. It remained her fenced-in play yard.

Because she was so small and the kennel so big, we placed pieces of a cardboard box to make a smaller enclosure for her outside the kennel for the first night. I could see our puppy wanted to run. The first thing she did was try to climb out. The sides began to fall over. That cardboard was not going to hold her back! We propped the sides up with books, realizing the next day we would have to put her inside the kennel regardless of her small size.

But for the first night, she would have to sleep in the small area we made for her. After pawing at the newspapers on the floor, she slowly walked in circles and just dropped in her tracks, spread out and went to sleep. Good girl! She closed her eyes.

About 1 a.m. I heard whimpering. It was a very faint sound. Momentarily, I had forgotten about the puppy, until I heard scratching on cardboard, along with the whining. I got up and went to check. I saw a little fur ball running around on the living room carpet. She had knocked over the wall and had crawled over the top. She was free! Mypsy's freedom would not work for me.

My Love was sleeping soundly, unaware Mypsy was running around. I needed to sleep. I had not thought she might keep me up nights! That puppy had to sleep, or at least be quiet, in a safe place.

I found my floor exercise mat and a light blanket. (Hot July meant A/C was on, and it got cool in the evenings!) I put them and my pillow on the floor, lifted our little puppy onto my tummy and lay on the mat, pulled up the blanket, and closed my eyes.

That didn't work. She was running all around on my tummy, trying to escape from under the blanket. I lifted her down on the floor beside me where my arm would enclose her, would hold her in place up against the side of my body. It wasn't long before she was quiet. She finally slept! We both stayed there until the early sunrise filled the room with light and heat.

But I couldn't do that every night.

When My Love saw the arrangement the dog and I had made, he immediately went to work to finish setting the kennel in place. He arranged it where it would remain, as my sister reminded me, on one of the most prime pieces of real estate in our apartment: right beside our big picture windows. From her front gate, she had a great view of the river; she would feel breezes when the door was open in spring and fall; and most importantly, she had easy access to the balcony for quick in-and-outs to the pee pads.

That location made sense right then while training her. She only missed going outside one time, just once. She did not understand the change from paper to pee pads. But because she was close, we were able to respond to her "bell ringing" at the door and could work with her easily from there. She learned quickly.

My Love was already smitten. I think he had loved her from first sight! This hard, stiff, routine man had fallen in love with the cutest little beating heart ever.

He wanted to feed her. So, he fed her. Three meals a day he fed her. He wanted to do it. He did it. In time she knew the schedule to the minute and came to him for meals. I wanted to take her on walks. So, that was the trade-off. I walked her; My Love still could remember to feed her.

We met many dogs on our walks. Our Miss Gypsy wiggled all over to see each dog. The big dogs would turn away from the little ball of energy racing toward them. Some tiny dogs were afraid of her. She found her friends among the mid-size breeds with similar energy levels. We met dog-people like we had met parents through their children years before.

In time I could tell My Love wanted to take Mypsy out for her run, too. She had to run to keep up! I suggested we trade days, or alternate morning and afternoon. I was reluctant to stop walking. But I could not walk alongside My Love. His stride was longer than mine; within a block I was lagging behind the two of them. I had some arthritis issues, such that walking became awkward, uncomfortable, and painful, so we seldom walked together. Resolved: My Love took the dog walking once a day.

I took my turn walking with her until I got sick. I felt horrible. Night sweats, headaches, muscle pains, with bronchitis, and flu for eight weeks. So, My Love continued the walking routine, but added my walk to his.

And when I recovered, he continued both walks with the dog because he "needed to walk to help with my COPD."

I never argued. He did benefit from walking. I could not deny him. It took years for me to get my walking strength back.

But eventually, each time My Love headed to the basket to get the leash, Mypsy ran to my side. Her walk with me was hard-wired in her brain; it seemed she felt I was the one who should be getting the leash and taking her for a walk. It was almost as if she were asking my permission to go with someone else. She asked before practically every walk, for years.

If I were in the bedroom, sick in bed, she'd run back there first. If I were in the kitchen, she'd come to sit in front of me to get my clap signaling "you can go." If I were typing, she'd sit beside me until I stood to walk her to the chair where she got hooked up.

I didn't make any of that happen. Mypsy created that routine on her own. My Love hated that she did it. When Mypsy would run to me, he got angry. He threw pillows at me. He told me I was encouraging the dog not to go with him. He threw the leash at me. Was he becoming a selfish child?

He'd yell at me, "I'm not going to take her out if she keeps running to you. She shouldn't have to ask you if she can walk with me." I had no idea how to make Mypsy stop. Nor did he. He couldn't be happy just with the fact that the dog went walking with him.

Had My Love become a jealous little boy or was he turning into a selfish fuddy-duddy, a grumpy old man? Or was this the beginning of slight dementia shifts I never recognized? My Love never understood it was the dog's decision; the routine had become ingrained along with her inner clock. He was sure I had engaged Mypsy in a conspiracy against him. He'd throw the leash and walk off. Strange.

I felt I was watching paranoia rising. Was he afraid I would prevent his beloved Mypsy from being with him? I never had.

"I'm not taking her if she won't come when I'm ready to go." His anger oozed out through his thinning body as he stomped off in a huff to get his jacket. He seldom saw the dog wagging her tail waiting for his encouragement for the hookup. All she needed was a nod and a smile without the energy of anger getting in the way.

My Love rarely understood the dog loved him. He just could not stand that Mypsy loved me. I never stopped the dog from being near him or walking with him. He believed I did. I felt I was watching a young child acting out, in need of attention. Had this become a recurring theme?

I suppose it was possible he had been unknowingly covering up his dementia tendencies one year before he had been diagnosed. I sure did not suspect his future, one year before his initial diagnosis.

If Mypsy was sitting by me on the couch, My Love would immediately move his false teeth, signaling an invitation for her to "come get kisses." He couldn't stand it when the dog jumped up on my side of the couch. He did not seem to understand our dog made the decisions on her own. She changed sleeping spots, taking little naps on different pillows and chairs. My Love wanted the dog to be by his side, to be his alone. I felt he resented sharing her. I never knew the trigger for that behavior, but then I really never knew where many of his idiosyncrasies originated.

So, My Love took Mypsy walking with him in the morning and afternoon. I never argued. Once they got through the hookup incidents, both were anxious to go. Both needed to walk outside. I didn't want an argument every day. So, I let it go. It was one way My Love felt he was being helpful, plus doing what he wanted to do.

They were good buddies. He adored her. He was with her on the balcony, in the living room, and on their walks. As the breeder had predicted, they had developed a lasting bond. Mypsy did hit it off with My Love, but always came back to me for permission and bedtime sleep.

Even with his need for having the dog to himself, I noticed their bond seemed to have changed My Love for the good. I perceived a much gentler person. Was the change from working with a smaller animal, another beating heart? For a brief period, he did seem to think of another being instead of himself. Big job for a little dog.

His illness came second to the dog. That was an unexpected outcome! My Love would opt to stay home to be with Mypsy instead of going with me to the store. He created his routine around her schedule, which eventually became their schedule. I learned they both had clock-watching, impatient personalities.

When My Love was diagnosed with Alzheimer's disease, it was a blessing to have Mypsy. She kept him on track. Walking her helped him with his need to be the social butterfly he used to be. She helped keep the schedules they shared.

At times, she went too far. By standing in the hook-up chair, she demanded he'd go walking. When she rang the bells, as we had taught her, she was demanding we let her outside. She'd stare My Love down when it was time to eat. And generally, he responded in the minute. So, in response, she became, even more, a little princess. But he loved our little boss even more.

It was fascinating to watch the two of them. My Love was, indeed, the master. I was Mama, substitute for the mother dog Mypsy left behind. When she was hurt or frightened, or she heard thunder or fireworks, she came to sit beside me or on my lap. When she wanted to play, she taunted My Love until he got up to run through the rooms with her. At bedtime, she waited for my arm signal so she could follow me to bed.

Each night she slipped down along my side, just as she had that first night, and slept. My Love would periodically sit up and check on her throughout the night. And in the morning when My Love began to stir, Mypsy knew it was time for her breakfast. She was up the moment My Love's feet hit the ground, flying like a squirrel, from atop the bed, across to the floor, in the hall. The two of them headed for the kitchen.

I had wanted a dog. Mypsy was far more than just a dog. She softened our lives, giving purpose to two seniors who otherwise would not have known the love she shared with us. Our puppy made us a family. Some days I was sure she was the only glue holding us together!

In the beginning, My Love's normal behavior relaxed. His sensitivities sharpened. I thought he seemed more content now with a dog in our life.

But then later, as his dementia progressed My Love's anger started to show up in many areas of his life, including the relationship between the three of us, Mypsy, My Love, and me. And it was not such a pleasant period for any of us.

I know Mypsy provided an incentive for My Love to get up each day, to stay as healthy as he could for as long as he could. My Love's dog walking kept him in the best physical shape of his life, until his seventy-ninth year, when walking became difficult! He walked her up through to the day before he went into the hospital.

But when My Love's calcium elevated, his leg muscle pains prevented their time outside for several months. Walking with Mypsy had been a successful deterrent to his advancing COPD, but he could not walk with knee pains. Hospital stays were said to take a toll on seniors. My Love never again walked his thirty blocks a day after he came home.

As dementia and My Love's other tag-along diseases progressed, and his pains increased, Mypsy was no longer getting her walks every day. When they did go out, My Love was not always remembering the by-law to poop and scoop. The fine for failure to obey was high, but my love did not relate. It was important that I remind him every walk.

Mypsy did not understand. She would sit in front of My Love and whine to go outside! After all, our pet knew what time it was! So, I began to walk with her when I was still able to leave My Love for a short time. Their walking days were over while My Love was in pain. I guess I was a caregiver for Mypsy, too. As they say, I was speaking for those who couldn't speak for themselves. In time, that applied to both My Love and Mypsy.

I know for sure that, like Will Rogers, I want to go to the same heaven where Mypsy will be. She was the sweetest little dog, a gift for both of us.

12 TRUSTED CONFIDANT

It never was my intention to be My Love's secretary.

One day, I learned the history of the role. Even as far back as 600 AD, a secretary was a "keeper of secrets, someone who handled tasks of a sensitive nature." It was a position of honor, distinguished by trust. So now, if I felt I had necessarily become a secretary of sorts, I told myself I had undertaken something very important. I was trusted.

My Love and I worked together for nearly eighteen years before we retired. It was widely known that we had separate functions. He was the president. It was his company long before I came on board. I was a salesperson and eventually became their marketing manager. I deliberately was not in an advisory role.

We did work together on international projects and then again when I was designing and editing the company's website. But rarely at other times. Independence was not new to either one of us. We did our own thing, during work, plus a lot in our own time. And later, after we got together, we continued the "do our own thing" routine, even at home.

So, after carrying that mindset for years, I had to adjust when I realized I would become his assistant, his secretary. Once we were retired, and his string of diagnoses began to increase, I began scheduling his appointments on the calendar, keeping up with this life. He just couldn't do it. Slowly, I adapted to his need for help. Later, he relied on me one hundred percent to be there.

~

"That cough of yours!"

I mentioned his annoying rumble, his cough progressively catching in his throat. Since we spent more time together after our retirement, I noticed it increasing with each day.

"You really need to see your doctor about it," I said. He looked at me with a furrowed brow, that "you have no business telling me to see a doctor" look. It was just like he used to look at me when I dared suggest something for his company. I knew he meant that it was his decision. But he had done nothing about his coughing for years. He ignored it. I was tired of hearing the rumble in his chest.

I risked mentioning his cough, but he didn't seem to want to hear anything about it. Maybe he sensed within himself that something was not right.

Finally, he responded when I asked.

"I don't have a doctor."

There. It came out. A response I should have suspected. But My Love's private-self never shared his medical world, doctor, diseases, none of it, with me. So, I finally discovered he hated going to doctors.

I had not realized he didn't get checkups, never updated vaccinations, and never went for flu shots. Same with dentists and optometrists. But in all our years, it never occurred to me that he would not have a doctor relationship established! Why wouldn't he want someone to care for his health?

From our local hospital website, I wrote down names of the few doctors taking new patients. My Love must have been blessed with a wee bit of luck. A young doctor had recently opened a practice in a health centre not fifteen minutes from our home. And he would take My Love as a new patient. Grateful.

In a foreshadowing of years to come, I began to schedule My Love's many appointments, to keep track of his appointments, to understand and enforce preparations needed. I became the taxi to his appointments. I took notes during his appointments.

I learned he was not comfortable arranging or being responsible for any of it. How did that happen? He used to do it all, or so I thought.

I finally had to fill that role, the one I had avoided at all costs! His secretary.

But inside, I knew I had finally become his trusted confidant.

13   AFFECTING US BOTH

"Why did you just pound the arm of the couch? What made you so angry?" I finally was able to ask without seeming too annoyed.

But, of course, My Love seldom could explain his anger. Usually, by the time I asked, he had no idea what he had done and certainly not why. He was not in control. I always felt his anger came from an inability to comprehend his diseases. I was probably wrong because that would imply that he understood. Dementia would not allow that.

Over time, I had learned losing his temper was part of his increasing frustration. I had to "be aware and take care" while realizing it wasn't his normal behavior, although very real. Most times he had emotional anger, but sometimes he expressed anger physically, hitting the couch or raising his arms in the air. He didn't touch me. But, when he was behaving in an unusual manner, who knew what changes could emerge? I did not want to become a casualty.

At some point, I felt the need to manage his medication. I worried he might forget to take a new pill because it was new to his routine. He wanted his familiar medicine. I had to step in. He could get loud, even angry, or wrinkle up his face and scowl toward me when I tried to help.

"I've always taken my medicine," he reminded me, in not such a nice way. "I don't need your help. I can do it myself," said my seventy-nine-year-old child!

Maybe he thought I was limiting his independence. But he was forgetting what pills he had taken and when. It never was easy telling him my monitoring related to his memory loss. He thought I was lying to him. How did I get around that underlying distrust that was building? He seldom believed me. He had *anosognosia*, described as when a loved one is unaware of their decline; has limited ability to understand their illness; is unmindful that any illness even existed. Go ahead, Google it. I had to!

I tried putting the old bottles away in a box. He got mad. I tried throwing out his old pill bottles. He dug through the trash to retrieve them. *Accidents* could happen, and I did not want improperly dispensed medication to be cause for an accident. We compromised. I monitored from the hall, and he tried not to become upset. Inch by inch we worked with the issue of the moment.

I had rarely seen much anger in My Love before. Even so, his current emotions were different. His new anger was unpredictable and felt mean. I had to be aware and take care. In time, My Love was taking his anger out on me, yelling at me more than before. Was he reacting to his perceived loss of freedom? I suspected years of being self-sufficient meant a long transition period between denial and acceptance. Was that it? Was he beginning to accept his memory loss? Probably not. He never acknowledged anything was wrong, especially if I asked him. He truly had anosognosia.

I was confused. How should I react to his unexpected change in behavior? I had never taken an anger management class, and obviously, nor had he! I was not sure such a class would work at this stage. I preferred the idea that he might be angry, acting-out, because he had his diseases. I could only hope it wasn't personal.

But I was having trouble holding myself back from just exploding, letting it all out, yelling my frustrations at the same volume he was putting his out into the room!

I mentioned My Love's anger to the young physical therapist who came to help him after his second hospital visit. She happened to be here during an ad on the TV for St. Jude's Hospital. She told me I had to persist. If those children could smile so brightly, I had to rise up, I had to smile. I had to keep my mind on my caregiving.

My Love's therapist was coaching me! When the ads came on TV, I related to them and My Love smiled. A smile usually defused any situation. I reinforced that understanding with my new support, My Love's therapist.

Who is more frustrated? Come on. Let's argue! I can't keep silent forever.

My Love and I were both near the ends of our ropes. I just hoped we could wrap that rope around us and tie lots of knots to hold us together!

I was having trouble moving beyond that personal moment and into the realm of an impersonal caregiver, where I needed to be.

Just keep smiling!

His occasional outbursts were erupting with more frequency over the weeks. It was not that easy for me just to wave them off. I hated that I had to get used to his flare-ups without feeling personally attacked. I hated when I felt my thoughts turn to anger. Maybe if I ignored his behavior toward me, his anger would stop. Of course, that could not happen, he was acting without forethought.

I wanted to respond unkindly, verbally, out loud, just like he did!

Why do you get to yell, and I am supposed to keep quiet?

My inner child was alive and well! No intellectual discussion was going to take place. Not then, at least.

I felt like I had been cornered, too. How could anything be resolved? How was I supposed to be the adult in the room? Count to ten? Even saying "one" was difficult, just so that I could get to ten. But over time, I realized I had no choice.

In due course, the frequency of outbursts accelerated. I began to wonder how his outbursts might be tied to the sundowning syndrome. He would be angry, aggressive, borderline hostile, not quite physically abusive. And when it would end, unbelievably, he'd behave as if it never happened. He'd settle and was no longer angry. What had happened? It was impossible to know when the episode would end or what his personality would be like at that point.

My Alzheimer Society counselor suggested a strategy for handling this sort of situation. Count as high as I could so that I could get past the need to respond with angry words. One thousand two, one thousand three . . .

Great! But first, I had to recognize I needed to count!! I was coming in a beat too late! My Love's anger nudged my anger on the first beat of the first bar of the opening stanza. His music began before I knew we were going to play!

Another suggestion was that, before I reacted, I should take the time to ask myself if my response was being helpful or hurtful? Too late. I couldn't wait that long! I was already pushing back. No, I could not get these new ideas going for me. Maybe it was months or even years too late for me to be a successful caregiver at this level! But I had to persevere! No time to rest.

One suggestion I thought might work was meditation. I had used meditation many times to sort out issues when I needed to feel the answers. But when I tried meditating, too much thinking was in the way, I just couldn't find that quiet mental space. I kept trying. By the time I felt I was overwhelmed in my caregiver role, some said I had just run out of steam. Too late. Others said I was close to crisis myself. I had no way to know I had advanced that far.

It made me wonder, *Who monitors caregivers?*

There was no talking anything out with anyone. I began needing help with my anger as much as My Love did. Knowing intellectually was one thing; being detached enough to be disciplined was quite another. I was in way over my head! And no one else realized it. I had no choice but to keep smiling. I knew no other way.

~

That day at the doctor's office My Love was given a paper to fill in. He rolled the paper and was going to put it in his pocket. I could tell he did not understand he was to complete it right then, so I asked if he wanted me to help write the information for him. Typically, he was receptive when I offered.

This time, when I asked, he elbowed me. "You just shut up!" he said as he pulled away and walked on to his seat in the waiting room.

Oops! Did my words offend him in a public setting? Did I embarrass him because he rolled the paper? No one was watching. But I was left with remnants from those angry words.

"You don't want my help?" I asked again.

As he shook his head no, he folded the paper and put it in his pocket.

My Love seldom had spoken such abrupt words to me, but his miserable attitude was running parallel to his progressing Alzheimer's disease. Everything was getting worse.

I wondered, *What next?*

I could feel that his frustrations were right below the surface. And lately, I recognized that my own situational frustrations were rising in response. I was having as much trouble holding back as he was. I didn't like how I felt.

If I wanted to be able to help him in future months, I could not be the recipient of angry words and be expected just to ignore him. It was like he got to release his anger, but I wasn't being given the same time in the ring. He got a pass because he was sick! I couldn't let it go! I needed relief as much as he did.

Although I knew I shouldn't, sometimes I'd just walk away and leave him. I agonized knowing I needed to become more disciplined with my reactions, but it was hard for me. My friends told me to go in the bedroom and pound the pillow, get away from the immediate environment. Sadly, pounding pillows did me little good! I really needed to find a quiet meadow, miles away, a place I could mellow out . . . for days . . . while the emotions dissipated! But there was no respite in sight!

Back at the doctor's office, without a word, I got up and walked out to the car to wait. Suddenly, I was overcome by an urge to move the car to another parking spot to see how My Love would react if he thought the car was gone, to see if he thought I had left him. What was happening to me? I soon realized that leaving the office had not dispelled my tension. I knew better, but I could not stop myself.

When did I forget it is sometimes better to react with no reaction?

Will he notice if I move the car? Will he care?

Would he know why? Did I even know why?

I was the one carrying the burden of emotional residue. He had no idea what was happening. And something not very nice was happening to me . . . and I almost missed it. I suppose I only needed some sign of appreciation! I felt my caregiver gig had become just a thankless job. I needed some spark of gratefulness. For years there never was a word of appreciation. Just expectation. How long would I continue to do something for someone who told me he didn't think I did anything for him? Someone who felt no gratefulness, who showed no gratitude?

I had heard there would never be appreciation. Until that moment I did not understand how hard that was. I was not an angel of mercy! Giving and giving and giving was a lot to ask.

Almost never hearing a *thank you* was one of the hardest things of the whole experience! Year upon year. Everything I did was expected, never appreciated.

What keeps me at it? Where is my breaking point?

As My Love moved into the moderate stage of Alzheimer's disease, his attitude changed. He would grab my hand and say, "Thank you." And then forget again. He gave me little hugs. He seemed more thoughtful in his moments of clarity. I was surprised that was possible in his declining state of dementia. I don't know what caused the switch, but he was kinder. Maybe he wanted to be sure I stayed close by. Or maybe his need to be mean had dissipated for a time. Either way, I could only hope. I knew nothing ever stayed the same. And it didn't.

~

There I sat in the hot car watching the exit door of the building. Of course, I knew I was wrong. I realized I had overreacted. How could I get a handle on my feelings? I felt sad watching the man I once knew changing, disappearing, but at the same time, I did not want to care for someone who mistreated me. I felt trapped.

I had become a woman I did not want to be, living in a situation I did not ask for, breeding resentment I did not want to carry with me.

I was angry, yes. Frustrated, yes. In a calmer state, I would have recognized I had gone too far. But I had not seen any flashing red flag for me to get help.

What do I do?

Thankfully, I had time to step out of the car and to go back inside. As suggested, this time I asked myself if my actions were helpful or hurtful. But then I still couldn't let it go. I asked, "Helpful or hurtful to whom?" Resentment was not that easy to shake off!

I arrived in the waiting room just as My Love was coming out of the examination room. He smiled. The fact that I had left earlier never was mentioned. I'm sure he did not remember.

He went alone to make his next appointment and handed me the reminder card. I said nothing, not wanting to stir the pot. We walked to the parking lot, where I had parked the car in an entirely new location. I'm not sure he remembered where we parked in the first place. I will never know. I did not ask.

But it was right that I had left the office; I had to breathe, to think . . . alone. I took myself away from that space, partly so I would not react further to My Love's angry words and action toward me. If I could not find a way to ignore his anger without pushing it inside me, without becoming angry myself, I wouldn't be able to continue being his caregiver. My emotions were coming on strong and I had to handle them.

Those were the early years. If I could let go of my need to make an angry response before I acted, maybe it would work out as years progressed. It seemed My Love could not stop his frustrated and agitated behavior. Intellectually, I knew I had to end mine. But there was much more to it than that, I was sure. A scenario I would have to bring up with my Dr. JohnTwo at the psychotherapy clinic. Could it all be unraveled?

~

Follow-up after meeting with my Alzheimer Society counselor and with Dr. JohnTwo:

"Breathe! Count to the highest number necessary. Be still. Refocus. Breathe. Listen to the breath."

My doctor even suggested I ask myself if the situation and my response were more hurtful than helpful. I just kept thinking, *To whom?* It was not easy to keep telling myself I needed to change so that my own emotions would calm down amid the changing, increasingly stressful lives we now led. My emotions needed a release, too.

In the end, I knew intellectually that during a state of calm all these emotions could be quieted. All I could do was to keep working on my responses, even if it seemed I was losing the battle.

Sometimes, breathing was not enough. Punching pillows didn't work. Counting to one thousand was not high enough. Meditating took more time than I had. So, I purged, creating volumes of written words. But nothing was enough to remove my pains inside.

~

In time, after his first two-week stay in the hospital, I noticed more of My Love's behaviors changing. I noted after being home for two months, his dementia seemed to slide much faster. I couldn't ask him to get me anything because he'd forget why he had gone before he reached the destination. He'd look at something and have no idea what he was to do with it. He'd easily forget what he had just said. Memory was fading at all levels. Interpreting his nonverbal expressions as conversation was new for me.

Much of his tendency toward anger did not reappear at that time. Only later was I introduced to sudden bursts of anger that came out of nowhere. But I am getting ahead of myself and his story.

During that first hospital stay, the doctors had taken him off several of the medications because of what they called reactions to medications. He'd been taking those meds for several years. Were all those unfamiliar behaviors in response to the medications? We would never know. I was told there would be too many tests to find out and no one wanted to put him back on the meds to check it out.

Not long after he was home from the first hospital stay, he developed pain in his knees, legs, groin, and lower abdomen. Those pains increased and became the next hospital focus. His high calcium levels were playing games again. Then his anxiety episodes and those dreaded sundowning moments reappeared after the second hospital stay. Why was My Love's life always so remarkably complex?

Following each hospital stay, I brought home a new person I had to get to know. For a long time I had to endure by the "live one moment at a time" philosophy. I couldn't even make it one full day.

14 HANDLING MONEY

"I'll get that," My Love said as he reached to take the bill from the waiter.

Then, putting it back down on the table, he took a roll of cash from his pocket and started counting out twenties. I gently pushed on his hands to suggest he do that somewhere else.

He squinted his eyes, sending darts toward mine, indicating, "not your business." He loved carrying money in a roll in his pocket, generally a roll of two one-hundred-dollar bills and some fives, tens, and twenties. In his earlier years he probably carried five hundred dollars at any one time. But when he flashed his roll of bills, to me he seemed like a gangster, and I became uncomfortable.

And now that he was a senior with Alzheimer's disease, he unknowingly joined the ranks of target for criminals. Someone with an inclination toward knocking off some old guy with a wad of cash in his pocket, someone who happened to see him paying the bill, could have marked My Love for a hit-job in a dark parking lot.

I wanted to eliminate that temptation for anyone. I wanted to avoid disaster. Because he had Alzheimer's disease, I began to worry about the money issue. I had to be creative in how I talked to him about it without arousing a war that I would not win. It was his money to lose, after all. But that attitude was irresponsible for me as a caregiver, not to mention as his partner!

I even noticed My Love bringing out a roll of cash from his pocket when he paid a check under ten dollars for a round of coffees.

Although My Love's ability to add and subtract in his head was diminishing, he wanted to be the sole controller of his money. Not that he had a lot, but if we weren't smart, he'd have less.

He usually could use the ATM machine. But I noted he started going to tellers when he began to forget his password. Most of the time he recognized the difference between a five-dollar bill and a ten. Maybe it helped that Canadian bills were different colors. But I saw his confusion rising considerably and I had to be ready to intercede in a nice way. I kept experimenting with strategies.

We went together to talk to a representative in his bank about the proper approach to the subject of money for one with memory loss, only I had to be careful in my wording in front of My Love.

He had a strong opinion that he could handle his own money without help. After a short meeting, it was concluded that since he had demonstrated he could think clearly about money, he still could oversee his checking account. We decided to put a limit on his account of the amount of money he had access to through his debit card. We put a daily limit for any withdrawals.

His routine had been to get his monthly allowance after his pensions were deposited. Nothing changed there. He could carry a limited amount of money because he could access only a limited amount of money. It worked, and I hoped it would for months ahead. He still could access his money.

In time he did not keep up with the cash in his pocket. I'd find it on his dresser or tucked in his billfold and he didn't remember it was there. He would not let me go into his bank with him. Even though both names were on the account, he seemed to feel I was going to take his money.

One day when going through the drive-through at my bank, I asked if he needed some cash. When he said yes, I took it from my account and handed it to him. He had no idea where it came from. He never thought to ask. Later that day I transferred that money from his account to mine online. Another strategy that worked without any angry words.

I must admit, his life-long practice of carrying a roll of money in his pocket was a concern of mine, even before his diagnosis. He liked to help pay for something I wanted when he could. I suggested he reduce the value of the bills in the roll. I provided fewer and fewer over time. To my surprise, he went along with the idea. And soon after that, he didn't know.

My goal was to get him to put a couple tens in his wallet and nothing in his pocket. In the end, he did reduce to three twenties in his billfold. He didn't need money, but he wanted to feel he had some. Occasionally, he would check for money in his billfold when I told him we were going out, even to visit friends. Eventually, he forgot he had those twenties in his wallet.

In the beginning I had not considered money would become an issue until one time when he was paying the bill when we were out to dinner.

We were with friends. We had a great visit, feeling happy, chatting during our meal. The bill arrived and, in the way he had done many times, My Love reached to take the bill from the waiter. He opened the folder and looked at the bill. I could not see the total. I certainly did not want to embarrass him to ask if I could help. Being one of the first times I had encountered bill-paying as an upcoming issue, I was not prepared with words to use.

Our friends were watching as My Love appeared to be trying to figure out . . . he seemed to be thinking, taking a bit more time than usual. Was he proofing the bill? Was he figuring out the tip? That would be OK, but he seemed to have a glazed look in his eyes. I thought he didn't know what to do next; perhaps feeling too embarrassed to ask for help.

"Can I leave money for the tip?" I whispered. He nudged me as if to say, "Stay out of this." I could tell he was confused and had no idea what he was doing. The waiter appeared, and My Love handed him the folder with several different colored bills inside. Again, I was not able to see.

When the waiter asked if he wanted change, My Love said, "No. It's ok."

That was that. He seemed to have solved his inability to figure out the tip by just putting money in the folder and hoping it was right. Typically, I would not have even given paying that bill another thought. But this was a new topic I was going to have to strategize before for the next time we dined out.

As we were leaving the restaurant, the waiter came to me and handed me a ten-dollar bill. I asked what it was for and he just said, "The gentleman overpaid."

I thanked him, put the money away, and joined the group outside on the sidewalk. We were fortunate, especially since I had no idea what the payment should have been. Another waiter might have kept the full payment. But without this waiter returning the ten dollars, I would not have seen the situation for what it was. I wondered if the waiter realized he had helped me grasp what was going on, My Love's inability to calculate the bill and add a tip. I reflected. I had taken appropriate steps at the bank. I had been considering what would happen if he spent all the money in his pocket. I was considering if someone tried to get money from his account through the ATM. But I was not sure what to do about paying bills. And then I just decided to let it go. If he used all his money, which was no more than sixty dollars at a time, he would lose sixty dollars. So be it.

I knew that was a lot of money, but in the bigger picture of what he could lose, it was acceptable for his financial independence, as it were. He would not be able to get more if I took him to the bank. No one could make him take out more because of the withdrawal limit. He could pay for one dinner, and that would be it.

I could envision scenarios of someone attacking a senior. But I really could not dwell on that. I could not prevent that. He could still be attacked even if he carried no cash. So, I let the worry go. I have not thought much about it since.

Money became an issue when he went to the doctor or hospital and had to remove his pants. I asked if he would leave his money at home, so it wouldn't be a worry. He chose to let me put it in my purse while he was in a procedure or examination. He remembered his money was missing when he went to pay for a drink or lunch, but otherwise seemed to forget about it.

At times, I kept his money for days before he realized it was missing.

A couple years later we were attending an annual Alzheimer Society-sponsored dance. He had lost nearly sixty pounds in the past year. His clothes were baggy on him. But he had not wanted to try them on before the dance, so he wore them.

"The baggy, pleated look," I said.

When we got home, he hung up his clothes. I was in the kitchen and heard thrashing in his closet. He was upset. He could not find his billfold. He could not recall when he had seen it last. He looked in all his coats, in his pants pockets. On his dresser. In the bathroom, the usual places we looked when things went missing. He even looked places he had not been recently. No billfold.

I got dressed and went down to the basement parking garage to see if he had lost it in the car, in the front seat or under the seat or maybe even on the way to or from the car. No billfold. I did find an inhaler beside the seat, the one he had lost the night before. But no billfold.

Back in the apartment I asked him what was in his billfold. In his panicked state he was having a hard time thinking. He began to name cards off to me. His senior's card. His coffee card. His health card. A business card from a friend. That was all he could think of. He had no credit cards. He had no gas cards.

Even though he couldn't, I relaxed. The only card there I worried about was his health card, and we could go report it and get a new one the next morning. I went on getting ready for bed. Not worth losing sleep over. He was so upset he began having another episode. He couldn't breathe.

Nooooo! I was tired. I wanted to go to sleep. I found his breathing device and gave him a little green pill for under his tongue. I went to sleep. A bit later, I peeped through one eye and saw he was sleeping quietly. Thank goodness.

Later, I was awakened by the light on in his bathroom. I got up and went to turn it out. As my hand reached for the switch, I noticed, up on the shelf, turned up on end, behind his nose spray, his wallet. The folded brown leather billfold we had been looking for frantically for an hour. He was sleeping, so I put it where it normally would have gone at night, on his dresser. Peace.

On reflection, I realized that without much money in My Love's wallet, without anywhere to spend it, perhaps he would be free to handle money in a limited manner as his needs lessened. It seemed we could resolve this issue without making him feel a loss of independence.

I wondered if he ever figured out that he had nothing in his billfold worth his anxiety attack. I never brought it up. But at least I knew.

 **15** NO DRIVING

"No one is going to take my driver's license away from me!"

My love was reacting to the facilitator in the first class we had taken with the Alzheimer Society. A class where, in one four-week session, we were given an introductory overview of our life ahead.

The Alzheimer Society offered classes to those caregivers and loved ones with a dementia disease. Among them were classes designed just for family members to increase their understanding and, many times, acceptance.

Our introductory class gave us a sense of the support we would get from the Society in years ahead. In addition, it helped us understand some of the new emotions we were experiencing since My Love had been told he had Alzheimer's disease. Anger. Sadness. Fear. Hopefulness. Embarrassment. I felt them all, but never was sure My Love understood. I wanted to get beyond those feelings.

Our once-a-week classes offered brief overviews, such as how the diseases might progress over time based on the physiology and the specific areas of the brain affected and

- what services the Society offered to assist loved ones and caregivers as the disease progressed. A more intense class about the specifics of the disease came later. Each class introduced additional services available and

- what to expect from various community services, showing how the Society went beyond their scope to serve.

- Self-care for the caregiver was also included. A proposed program to keep the caregiver healthy and capable of handling the tasks of the stressful role ahead was something I referred to long after the class.

- There were legal aspects to consider as well, such as getting everyone thinking about the realities of the future.

Among the topics describing how this new disease might restrict abilities to do certain functions in daily lives was the discussion about driving. No one wanted to give up their license, everyone agreed. When the facilitator asked each person to give a reason why it could be something to consider, most were reluctant to say much at all. But, later in the discussion, the class members responded with a sense of understanding and submission, indicating an acceptance of their disease.

All except My Love.

His response was not just a comment. He was mad. Sitting beside him, I could feel the intense negative energy rising.

"Who says I can't drive? Who will take my license? You?" he asked the facilitator, ready to leave the room. He was seriously agitated. In just weeks after learning of his diagnosis, My Love seemed to be feeling his potential loss of independence . . . and nothing had happened yet. His readiness to jump on that topic always made me wonder if he had detected he had memory loss long before he was diagnosed. If true, I could understand he might have been thinking of consequences much longer than I had.

Others saw his reaction. The facilitator must have seen this reaction before. She reassured him she would not take his license. But I was more concerned about the residual energy that would spill over into his thinking and discussions at home.

As soon as we got home, My Love went to the balcony and sat in the cold for a long time before saying a word.

"Can they really take my license? I'm not going to those classes again," he said.

He had been thinking about it since the morning class.

"Your doctor has to recommend it," I reminded him. "The Alzheimer Society does not take your license away."

I explained the Ministry of Transportation, the people who issued a driver's license, would deny his application for a new license if a doctor suggested he didn't meet the criteria for driving or if they felt for medical reasons, he shouldn't be driving. The logic of safe driving that involved the driver, passengers, and others on the road was not going to be discussed. He would never have the capacity to understand.

"Well, I have my van. They can't take that!" he said defensively.

He was right. They wouldn't take his van. The Ministry would just not issue a license for him to drive. And I wondered about the vehicle license. I never got a chance to ask. I wondered who would report his driving abilities. His doctor never rode in the van with him. How would he know? His Memory Clinic doctor had never been in his car with him driving, either. It was going to be up to me to report him to his doctors. What a horrible burden to put on a caregiver. Yet I knew it was for the good of every-one, drivers, pedestrians, and My Love. I worked on getting that concept into my head. I hated having to do it.

I guess I worried about it a lot, because the Universe came to my rescue.

One day when My Love was driving up the ramp of our underground parking garage, the rear axel on his van broke in two. The rear end of his van dropped to the concrete. It was going nowhere. The van had to be trucked to a repair shop.

We found later the axel appeared to have been broken in one spot already, like the van had hit a sharp object at some point before, and it had continued breaking. Luckily, the final break happened without anyone being hurt. Whatever it was, My Love's vehicle was deemed unsafe and undriveable! Both he and his vehicle were going nowhere.

My Love could not afford the repairs. I did not have the funds to offer him. So, he sold his van to the repair garage. I was relieved. I did not have to say a word to anyone. Grateful.

When he was in the Memory Clinic the following winter, he was the one who advised the doctor he had not driven for several months because he had sold his van.

Although he still walked, he could not walk everywhere. He had not yet taken the bus or the taxi.

He did not know about the van especially for those with special needs. I wanted him to like the train, but he resisted. For every place he had to go, I was his preferred on-demand transportation. I had some work to do to introduce new ideas and new ways to get around!

But there. It was done. He told the doctor. The doctor told the Ministry. A month or two later My Love received a letter from the Ministry asking for his driver's license. By that time, he had not been driving for some time.

Thankfully, the Universe found the smooth transition to no driving.

16 SOCIAL EXERCISE

"Stretch! Release! Stretch! Release!"

We were late to class but heard the instructions coming into the hallway from the multipurpose room where we always met for our exercise-social time. We hurried to find free seats and sat to catch our breath.

"Stretch! Release!" I heard again. Then I noticed everyone was seated. I had expected to see arms outreached, or legs in the air. But curiously, no!

And then I saw it. The little rubber ponytail hairband each person had around their fingers, which stretched as participants opened their fingers. I knew hand exercises were important, I'd been doing them for years to keep my autoharp-playing hands nimble. The hair band was a great prop for our overlooked hands.

"Stretch!" I watched everyone spread their fingers open against the force of the band. "Release!" And hands went down.

Just as I understood the exercise, a volunteer appeared, handing My Love and me a clothes peg.

"Pinch! Release! Pinch! Release!"

I looked around. We had missed three classes while My Love had been in the hospital and we were now catching up on what the others had learned. The clothes peg was to be pinched between the thumb and other digits as exercise for the fingers, cycling through each hand twice.

"Ouch!" The ring finger was tough for me at first.

"Keep trying," said the lady next to me. Someone new to meet!

Quickly, I realized we had almost missed the first exercises of the class, two new ones that preceded the main routine which normally started by marching in place in our chairs.

We had heard for years that continued mental and physical exercise was good for everyone, but we knew it was especially important for those with dementia and their caregivers. Add to the equation that many caregivers and their loved ones were also seniors and the need for exercise increased. The value of this class always seemed huge. Not to mention the social advantages. It made us feel good physically and mentally.

No matter which dementia diagnosis a loved one had, a better quality of life emerged for both the caregiver and the loved one when their lives included exercise and socializing.

~

"Pick a number. There are eight exercises." We each took a card with a number on it from the basket and gathered in our number groups.

During the first day of each ten-week session, the leader directed our attention to the eight initial testing exercises that would create the baseline for evaluating our personal benefits gained from being in class.

"March in place for thirty seconds." Coaching a caregiver, one volunteer held a timer in her hand, counting leg lifts. "Your knee must reach the level of the tape on the wall as often as possible." That was hard for me after the timer reached twenty-five seconds! The coach cheered us on as she counted the steps.

"With the weight in your hand, bend your elbow and lift your hand to your shoulder, and then next, do the same in your left hand. Count lifts with me." We were being timed! Eight. Nine. Ten. What was next?

"On 'go,' walk up to the tin can on the floor, circle around it and come back to this chair. Walk as fast as you can." Some members zoomed around the floor. I got there but struggled to keep my balance. My combination of speed and balance needed some more work!

At the end of the sessions, in nearly every case, there was significant improvement when tested again. After ten weeks in one one-hour session a week, it was good to see how much improvement participation in that class produced. My Love always improved. He loved the activity.

It was helpful for loved ones to have their "personal trainer" with them, usually a spouse or an adult child, a sibling, or possibly a paid professional caregiver. Volunteers helped in each class as well, doing the exercise as examples for us to watch.

We all went through the workouts led by a trained fitness instructor, who presented a program for adults with reduced abilities. She talked to us as she demonstrated what to do. She had us count along with her, taking our attention away from our groaning muscles and making the hard moments pass quickly. Six. Five. Four. Three. Two.

The exercise phase was similar to an Aqua fit class at the Y. In this exercise-social time, we had no water, no bathing suits, but instead we had lots of people in runners ready to move their bodies, seated on chairs and tapping their feet to the beat of the music and following the voice of the leader.

Throughout the class we stretched our arms and legs, we tightened our abs. We pulled, we pushed, we reached, we sat, we stood. We squeezed our knees and, aided by rubber balls and stretch bands, we enhanced our movements. We moved our fingers, gathered the wide stretch bands, rotated our hands and arms. We lifted and shrugged our shoulders to correct our posture.

Important especially for seniors, we improved our balance weekly by putting our feet toe-to-heel while holding on to the chair; we eventually freed our hands from support while standing on our toes. We walked and marched through the halls. Well, in truth, My Love ran or walked quickly in the early years. As time went on, even walking was harder, until we no longer attended.

After an hour of successful movement, we were rewarded with a social hour, a game, a cookie, a coffee or tea—a time of getting to know new people. The second hour of the exercise-social time program focused on socialization, mental activity featuring group interaction and games. Usually, we were seated in small groups. Volunteers would start a game, perhaps asking each person to remember and share something about his life in some way, a great get-acquainted process.

At another time, picture cards were spread across in waterfall fashion. In turn, each person around the table picked a picture that they liked and were asked to share why they picked that card. Usually, each one picked a card representing a favourite activity from when they were young and then shared a memory with the group. Several times we explained how our card choice related to our current life. The tie-in, of course, for those with memory loss, was that "memory remembers early years more than recent years." They could still participate. Who knew an old memory from a new one, anyway?

My Love chose a picture for a story from his teen years, one about being a life guard at the beach. On his second round, he picked a picture about skiing and told of when he was a ski instructor. The third picture he chose reflected his walks with "his" little Mypsy, our dog! This activity provided as much mental motion for the brain as the physical hour of exercises had done for the body. Best of all, our social hour offered a platform for the group to become more acquainted.

Over time, we played many games. One memory game involved starting with a pile of chips! You picked a card from a pile and read it aloud. "Change a flat tire." Those who had not changed a flat tire put one of their chips in the middle. Those who had changed a flat tire took a chip from the pile. The one with most chips at the end of the game, won . . . a cookie!

Another game was a modified shoots and ladders type travel board game where each player talked about some place they had lived at each stop on the board. Or they answered a question from a card drawn from a pile.

The Hasbro game Jenga required more thought, coordination and focus, removing logs from a tower. In that game four players were teamed up, two by two at a table. Lots of laughter was heard as more holes were seen in the towers and the tension heightened. Then boom! Game over! The Jenga tower collapsed and tiles spread across the table.

The socialization was of great value, and at the end of the class, most of the attendees looked forward to returning each week to be with their new friends during exercise and socializing. It was wonderful for a caregiver to share an opportunity like this!

Our sessions for this program took place at a beautiful community and cultural centre in our town. On the way to the room where we did physical exercises, we passed by large and small quilts. Fabric art hung along the hallway walls. There were photographs that students took, framed and displayed.

Art projects from a ceramics class were grouped in a showcase with similar wall projects hanging nearby. We viewed paintings from current classes. We watched special shows installed throughout the year. When we went for our class walk, we took different routes, so we could see work on the walls we had not seen the previous week. What a special place we had for our class.

One of the most fascinating exhibits for me featured necklaces displayed in showcases. Nature-inspired designs were explained and presented in a sketch book. Beginning with drawings of a snail, for instance, as the source inspiration, we saw how the sketch translated into a graphic plan for the necklace by way of a computer program. The designs then became a complete physical piece through the process of three-dimensional printing, a snail necklace from sketches of a snail. I found the results exciting, just brilliant!

In the building there was a museum and gallery for paintings and showcases for jewellery, woodwork and sculpture, fabric art, and pottery. What a treat to watch these changes throughout the year as we attended our sessions. Caregivers and loved ones alike were treated to beautiful visions and museum-quality artwork while we kept our minds and bodies active.

After the ten-week exercise-social time program ended, nearly all the participants wanted to be in the following session. It was indeed a successful program by the Alzheimer Society.

We made friends by taking part in their many programs. It seemed to me that organization and socialization remained a constant in all they offered their clients.

17 MUSIC GAMES

"Our last exercise will be to walk through the halls to see the new exhibits on the walls. At the finish line, go inside the Older Adults room." Our workout leader had given her final instruction for the spring exercise-social session.

The incentive, of course, was coffee, cookies, and socializing once we got there. Everyone loved their social coffee break before the second hour of our weekly exercise-social program.

Seated in small groups around tables, we were ready to play. Cookies gone, coffee cups emptied. Quiet came across the room. Ready. This week Musical Squares was the program.

Cards, with song names instead of numbers in the squares, were handed out at the tables. Every so often the sound of someone whistling a tune recognized on a card broke the silence, or someone began humming a familiar song. And then another started singing. A well-liked game on the agenda!

Volunteers spread small plastic chips across tables for covering song names. The facilitator explained the game, very similar to regular bingo many already knew. Most folks nodded they knew of bingo and agreed they could catch on as we played. By then, members of the Alzheimer Society sponsored group knew the games we played were for fun, no matter what the rules were!

With one question, directed to the person beside me, the game began.

"Can you pick a number between one and fifty?" the facilitator asked. Was it an easy question to answer? Maybe not.

The lady next to me showed puzzlement as she slowly asked, "A number? You want me to say a number?"

In a room of twelve to fourteen couples, mostly seniors, fifty percent had various types of dementia, at different levels. There was an abundance of tolerance and caring from almost every person, in every activity, mental or physical. It was typical for questions and rules to be repeated or explained throughout the games. The volunteers and staff were rich with patience and understanding.

"Yes," came the answer. "A number between one and fifty." The facilitator was intent to see if the lady understood. She was hoping the player would say a number indicating which song from the list of fifty to play to begin our Musical Squares.

I glanced at My Love to see if he had a number in his mind. I am not sure he knew why we were waiting. His smile sent me no message. Still confused, my friend asked, "What number would you like?"

It became apparent to me that this question, which many of us might call easy to answer, was causing anxiety in one with Alzheimer's disease.

I watched as my friend looked briefly at her husband, not sure what her response was supposed to be, looking for some help with the answer. The facilitator re-phrased her question.

"Can you tell me a number smaller than fifty?"

Again, I saw anguish cross the face of the lady seated next to me.

But then she seemed to grasp the question as she smiled and said, "Forty-nine."

"Great!" came the response.

You could almost hear everyone breathe in unison, silently cheering that my friend's answer had come. She gave a big, warm smile in return, realizing she had succeeded in finding an answer on her own.

A band began to play song number forty-nine. A voice came from the CD player, singing the words from "Show Me the Way to Go Home . . ." Suddenly, practically in sync, the group began to sing along. It did not seem to matter that the singer did not have a familiar voice. Most folks enjoyed the moments of singing and swaying together. This group knew the words. Of course, they would; seniors would be the right age to have heard and sung this song in their younger years.

We began to hear the clicking of the little plastic chips covering the spaces on those cards that had the words "Show Me the Way to Go Home" in one of their squares. And so, the game went on.

Oldie songs like the well-loved Irish tune "Danny Boy," the tweedily-tweedily-deet from the 1950s "Rockin' Robin," and Teresa Brewer's recognizable "Music, Music, Music" brought the group together singing along. It became evident that singing and enjoying the songs were equally important as covering a row of names and getting a bingo!

Mostly the songs played were from the 1940s, '50s, and '60s. "Tennessee Waltz," "That's Amoré," and "Mother" were familiar to most in the room. "Amazing Grace" received the biggest response. Voices across the room carried on long after the CD song selection stopped. It was clear many knew and loved that favorite.

We heard many older songs. "Side by Side," made popular by Kay Starr in 1953, "Heart of My

Heart," featuring the Four Aces in 1953, and Bobby Darrin's 1960s well known tracks "Mack the Knife" and "Beyond the Sea," were recognized, even if every one of the original artists were not the ones singing on the CD in our game! We played three rounds, with a "Bingo!" bringing each round to an end.

Any game with music was always a favorite, but Musical Squares appealed to all. It was suggested before the end of the hour that the developers of that game might include some Canadian content. There were U.S. marching songs, the U.S. National Anthem, and songs that seemed to be more American than Canadian. Our Canadians commented how they wished there was more Canadian songs in the game, and understandably! Maybe that could be a project for the future! I was having trouble thinking what songs they meant! I guess I thought of songs by titles, not nationality of authorship. Interesting.

The following session, the group of well-exercised caregivers and their loved ones again marched through the halls, along the way commenting on the new art pieces that had been displayed on the walls. The door to the Older Adults room stood open, welcoming the group, who were once again ready for their coffee and cookie break.

The tables and chairs had been grouped half on one side of the room and the rest on the other, with signs for each area, "Gents" and "Ladies." We were going to have a musical-sound recognition face-off!

Even seniors liked a respectable contest, guys against gals; this game excited the group. The competition, the intent listening, the group decision-making on what the sound was, working together until each group found their answer. The winning team guessed the most sounds correctly. They got the prize . . . cookies, of course!

"All quiet! Are we ready?" the leader looked at the volunteer captains on each side. "Here we go!"

"Men first." She looked at the "gents" table and played a sound. She always picked men first, at least we women thought so! You could see the men concentrating on the sound. Some thought they knew what it was, and some had no idea. They talked among themselves and came up with an answer and the volunteer reported to the leader.

"Dripping faucet," the volunteer called out.

"Right. Two points."

The men cheered and clapped. My Love caught my eye and gave me a thumbs up sign.

"Next, ladies, it is your turn. Try to guess this sound."

The leader played the sound. Again, there were those who recognized it and those who weren't sure. Someone whispered across the table that they thought it could be a chainsaw. Another shook her head in agreement. The volunteer gave the answer.

"Right. For two points. A tie!"

Then the ladies cheered and clapped. No woman wanted to give a wrong answer and let the men have a chance at a free point! So, the game progressed. There was an assortment of sounds, such as a running lawnmower, toilet flushing, phone ringing, bat hitting a ball, seagulls squawking in the air, train whistle, and many more.

There were a few sounds that some members found difficult to recognize. That day a squeaky door and a galloping horse stumped the players.

It always seemed to me that when there was music involved in the game, people loved playing. No one was judged on intelligence. No one had to be singled out to have to guess alone, enabling those with memory loss to remember those earlier life sounds with ease. It took team effort. A good feeling.

The pleasure of this second hour in our exercise-social program each week was in the laughter and fun that the members had together exercising and playing games. It was a safe place for those with dementia and their caregivers to have a social time, to feel reasons for happiness among others facing the same hurdles.

Winning was fun, but not serious. Everything we did was secondary to the social interaction. It was a time out of a day where those with memory loss could participate, could be equal to others in the room. It was a place where caregivers could relax, take a brief break and enjoy being with others, without judgment.

The games and socialization our Alzheimer Society of Halton provided represented some of the best ongoing support any caregiver could wish for!

18 STRINGS OF HAPPINESS

"Try and remain social as your lives move farther into the world of memory loss," our leader stressed. "You'll find you both will welcome the companionship and interaction."

They told us that isolation and lack of interaction were known to hasten dementia decline. We needed to stay engaged in order to give each person's life meaning.

Sounded like that might be true for anyone, with or without dementia!

During my intense and wide-ranging Alzheimer's disease education, I learned the importance of remaining social and cherishing my connections. Socializing stood out as a suggestion I hoped I could follow. But getting together with friends took planning and time; each came at a premium as we aged, and, indeed, My Love and I were aging, even as he moved along the memory loss spectrum.

Caregivers were encouraged to hold on to their social relationships from pre-Alzheimer's disease days. I was under the impression that those friendships would help balance any disappointments as memory loss increased or as friends dropped away.

However, life did not quite work out that way for me. Many of our former friends vanished over time. I continued to attempt contact with those I knew from before, but for countless reasons, keeping those connections became increasingly difficult. Going to lunch with retired friends was just one suggestion made to keep those former acquaintances active. I liked that idea because My Love and I both could be involved. It could be a "we" activity. In his early stage, I could go out alone. But as his dementia progressed, that was no longer as enjoyable. I found I was more focused on My Love back at home instead of enjoying the moment with a friend.

And, of course, not everyone we used to know realized that My Love had serious memory loss. I felt it was best to explain, but My Love wanted me to tell no one.

"I don't have anything wrong with me, why would you have to say that?" He would argue with me when I asked if I could mention his Alzheimer's disease. He felt when I told someone, I was not telling a truth about him. But for everyone's comfort, I learned to slip it in without his knowledge.

My Love became agitated when asked about his illnesses. He assured everyone he was fine. He thought he was.

When I explained to friends, I was relieved to hear, "Thank you for sharing that. It's hard to tell at first; he hides it so well!"

He did, at first. And then I finally figured out that when he realized he couldn't hide it very well anymore, he felt uncomfortable. He stayed quiet and let me talk for him. So, I kept telling friends that My Love might not seem the same person they knew earlier in life. Those who did not accept it were increasingly unavailable when invited to get together and silently slid out of our lives, or maybe we slid out of theirs. I did not chase those relationships. They were over. I had no energy to try to stay in touch. For what?

But there were some who wanted to stay in touch and get together, regardless. I was thrilled when we could see one or two former friends. It was never pleasant for My Love or me to watch friends fall away.

One couple we had not seen in almost ten years wanted to set an appointment for lunch following a reconnection through social media. My Love had worked with his friend for over twenty-five years before they retired. Early in our relationship, My

Love and I had met his friend's new wife and had taken them boating. We enjoyed their company, so, we were excited to meet for lunch.

"I don't remember their names. Do you?" My Love asked me, while we were waiting in the lobby of the restaurant. "What do they look like?"

He was telling me he would not recognize them by name or by sight.

I had to think about that. Most of our friends had gray hair, so not much distinction there. We knew men who were going bald or who had distinguishable facial hair. But I just tried to use descriptive words to create an easier picture for My Love to recognize someone.

"Last time you saw him he had lots of wavy white hair, with a full white beard," I explained, talking about the man who would join us.

Before I realized I might be confusing him, I went on, "He is taller than you are. He wore glasses that sat down on his nose a bit."

Way too much information, too fast! New habits were hard for me to form!

"Thanks! Lots of people in here look like that!" My Love responded, looking around at the people with grey hair and glasses already seated in the booths and tables.

I laughed. Seniors were everywhere!

I had never tried describing any friends to My Love, not in a manner I felt would help him identify individuals in a group. Plus, I had to use words he still understood. Boy, did I wish I had some ten-year-old photographs!

"Well, his wife is a petite lady. Not as tall as I am. She has a wee accent. I remember she had a sweet smile." I thought that might help to recall she was from Nova Scotia, or was it Scotland? "Her hair is short. It used to be blond," I added, knowing that was also common at our age. "It may still be blond!"

Like before, there were many petite blond ladies among those already seated.

Luckily, I had the advantage! I knew what they looked like; I would recognize them, I hoped, crossing my fingers. Indeed, I was able to spot them the minute they stepped through the front door.

I was not sure My Love was as convinced about the connection as I was. But once I bent toward them with arms open, waiting for a hug, he fell into his role, even with memory loss! He was able to carry on a limited, responsive conversation so well that few would have guessed he had not known his former friends right away.

"Ah, yes . . . You are right . . . Hmmm . . . Really? . . . Of course . . . I know that." Or he'd nod his head. Would anyone else know he was struggling to keep his illness hidden, that he was following his well-used scripts for cover?

My Love was not the first good actor I had witnessed among those with Alzheimer's disease! It almost seemed an ability or talent that came with the diagnosis!

He tried his hardest in every single conversation to make me think he was following, that he understood. He knew if he said something wrong it would make him look silly. He had told me, "I don't want to feel foolish." He had it all worked out. I wondered how long it would be before he forgot what foolish felt like.

Being with our friends, as we ordered lunch and talked about events we had experienced together, I realized I was being social, being invigorated. We laughed as if we had just been together yesterday. What a great time we had enjoying stories of years before, each of us inserting information the others did not quite recall.

I learned the value of grabbing those happy memory moments when we could so that we could string them together with other happy moments to make a happy day or happy week. I loved making strings of happy moments. They became magical soul food when I felt empty. It did not matter if the memories were recent or from years ago. The connection between friends made it special.

It was only a month after our lunch visit that I got an email from our friend's wife, saying her husband had been diagnosed with Alzheimer's disease and they probably would be staying closer to home. They lived about an hour away. Sadly, I knew some of what was ahead for them. I understood the hassle; I knew full well that, as time went on, things would change. The distance and the disease seemed too much for My Love to see his friend again. My Love was the one this time who decided not to visit. He was the one who knew he might feel uncomfortable. We never did get to walk with them along the lakeshore that summer. I just held on to the string of magical golden memories from years before. My Love had already forgotten.

I thought of the expression that went something like, "When one door closes, if you can't open it, find another to open elsewhere." I also had heard, "Stop banging on the locked door. It's not opening for you." So, we found another door.

The first year we were in the Alzheimer Society exercise-social time program, we met many new people. Typically, couples, a loved one with dementia and a caregiver, participated in the programs. That person could be a spouse, an adult child, a parent, a friend, and sometimes a paid professional caregiver.

Our new friends shared the common thread of memory loss and issues surrounding the care of loved ones. The compassion, understanding, concern, and kindness that flowed among those in the Society programs were feelings that streamed through those who put the program on and those who attended.

Between leaders, volunteers, and partici-pants, there was an atmosphere of acceptance that we felt prevailed throughout the Society, filtering through the programs they sponsored, blanketing all who participated.

Almost like a new family, we felt comfortable being together. And through the social part of their programs, through the active chair-fit sessions and Q&A game periods, we got to know one another.

When we no longer fit in with friends who were living their lives elsewhere, our Lifeliner Group, a by-product of the exercise-social class, was another door that opened. We were grateful for our lifeline friends who added much to our daily happy memory moments, who strengthened and added to our strings of happiness. Bless them all.

19 WEDNESDAYS FOR COFFEE

"Did you sleep more than six hours any night this week? I didn't!"

"I really need a hug! I have to go get tested for skin cancer again. Can you go with me?"

"You won't believe the hassle I got before we went to Seniors Social Club yesterday!"

"We had to get a rolling walker this week. She is just learning to use it."

"My Love gets upset if I monitor when he takes his medicines. But he forgets to take pills if I don't."

As members of our group arrived, they began their tales of the week. While putting their coat on the back of a chair before waiting in line to order their coffee, tea, latte, or sweet treat, they began their conversations as if they never ended the week before.

For over four years, our Lifeliner Group, a self-organized support group, met together to share and compare. Nearly every Wednesday we covered as much ground as possible in our ninety minutes together, including mandatory hugs all around.

During those years we had become lifeline friends, a Lifeliner Group. When we left after coffee, the other caregivers stayed in contact during the week to support each other at another meet-up. We lived too far and at that time I could not leave My Love alone for long. But our Group was amazing!

Note to caregivers: consider finding "caring people seeking caring people" to create such a group!

Members of our group attended the Alzheimer Society's exercise-social time when it was in session. But between sessions, we met at the Bakery Café for coffee during those same two hours. We knew what each one would order. We sat at the same two or three tables. Just like in elementary school, often we sat in the same configuration, in the same chair, week after week. Our discussions were serious and substantive, caring and helpful.

Our group was made up of five couples. Four women and one man were self-designated care partners for their spouses with memory loss. Five ladies seated snugly around one end of tables pushed together and five spouses sat around the other end. We learned that a group of ten was a good size for more personal discussions. Fewer people sitting at smaller tables meant everyone could be involved; no one was stuck on the end.

When we first got together, caregivers soon realized we had loved ones who were progressing along the dementia spectrum close to the same level. No one person had the exact dementia as any other. We learned from each other. Everyone was able to take part in discussions at some level, some more in depth than others. We were fortunate to have found compatibility among our new friends.

Our partners sat nearby, at the same tables, giving everyone an opportunity to socialize, to talk.

One wife found that her husband had become somewhat shy and quiet as his disease had advanced. She felt he needed to "be part of a conversation with other guys." He sat near the middle. Another man, who loved to be there, also sat in the middle on the opposite side. He smiled all the time and, at first, seldom spoke.

"But he is the one who reminds me we are going for coffee with our friends!" his wife told us. Every week they were usually first on the scene, arranging tables and chairs.

The tallest man, the caregiver, sat between the men and women. He sat near his wife, but also took on a unique role of bringing the other men into conversations. He realized the men, who had various degrees of dementia, were otherwise left to flounder in and out of meaningful topics. He brought his unique gift of inclusiveness to the other end of the table.

Our one male caregiver took on the role of not only talking with loved ones on their level, but also of being sure his own loved one, seated beside him, was involved in discussions with the women on the other side. As her illness progressed, his wife seemed to have become quieter and he felt compelled to give her the opportunities to be as social as she wanted to be. This same caring man explained to me how different his perspective of our group was because of the roles he took on. Until he mentioned it, I never gave much thought about a male perspective of caregiving. It did not occur to me his would not be like mine. I discovered how everyone experienced caregiving differently.

I hoped I was learning. I am grateful to the members of this group who helped me become more sensitive to the viewpoint of others, especially everyone who sat around that table.

Besides taking care of a loved one, each caregiver had issues of their own. One caregiver was struggling with breast cancer and an eventual double mastectomy at the same time she was taking care of her husband, who had recently had a heart attack. He had had a procedure to insert stents soon after. We all knew one consequence of anesthesia, sadly, would be increased memory decline. We experienced it with him.

Another caregiver had serious back issues. Pressure on her nerve caused severe pain, such that it was difficult to move at times. Still, she knew she must care for her husband, who had knee issues and blurred vision that was progressing, as well as Alzheimer's disease. We were concerned for her as much as for her husband.

My Love and I had become friends with these amazing people who lived role-model lives. Our group didn't just support those with dementia; we were supporting each other, the couple. We all knew the importance of a healthy caregiver. Our friendships proved to be priceless.

One spouse unexpectedly became a widow. Her husband had developed issues unrelated to his dementia. While he was in the hospital, he acquired an infectious disease from which he was unable to recover. Our friend relentlessly stayed by his side. After he passed, she spent time with her grief while trying to overcome her extreme burnout. Even while she was keeping depression at bay, she was always on our mind. Our friend spent time reviving her health while trying to deal with back pain. As she improved, she began to share her experiences to help others in the grieving process. We kept her close and when she could, she joined us at coffee or dinners.

She tried to be with others, knowing being social was important.

My issue was pain while walking, residue from years of myasthenia gravis. But I remained My Love's caregiver. At first, My Love's silence in the group made the others wonder when his memory would begin "to get lost." In that group, he wasn't his former social self. He spoke little. We couldn't tell where he was on the dementia spectrum. We couldn't tell what else was going on inside his body. Of course, he was the one pulling the wool over our eyes. He had the scripts down pat. Plus, he already had COPD and cancer before his memory loss diagnosis and was experiencing his anxiety attacks for the first times.

Alcoholics know their scripts. I supposed My Love would be considered an alcoholic, although never diagnosed. His long-term memory held onto those same scripts and they seemed to surface when he was in a dementia moment, a time when he knew he did not remember but had scripts to cover.

And then it seemed everything began to happen to My Love at one time. My weaknesses turned to exhaustion. I desperately needed respite, time I could put my caregiving responsibilities aside and think of other things. But, alas, dreaming as the clouds floated by would have to wait.

I did not get the provincial assistance the other caregivers in our group had because we lived in another district. When I was almost in crisis myself, help arrived. But that was a few years after our group got together. It was a blessing to have had others who recognized my situation and who were tuned-in more than I was at that time.

During the previous week, one of our loved ones had spent her first day ever at a senior day program. On that day, she spent a few hours with others in similar situations, accompanied by trained personnel who worked with them through the day. She was telling us how she felt after being there. The previous week she had explained she was hoping to go but was hesitant because she never had been before and would be going alone. We ladies had tried to assure her, if she did not like it, she would not need to go again. Of course, looking back I don't know if in saying that we were very helpful to her caregiver-spouse.

Fear was common. To me, trust and fear were opposites. Trust was built on memories, after all, memories of a safe feeling from the past. Caregivers dealt with issues of trust, fear, and forgetting every day. Forgetting meant forgetting everything, some things, a few things, and in no order and with no guarantee anything would be remembered or forgotten, including trust.

While telling us about her first day, a smile settled on her face.

Slowly, she told us, "It was organized. They had activities like our exercise-social time, with a few games." She was particularly happy telling us about her lunch. "They served wonderful beef stew with succulent beef and carrots."

Her specially chosen words reflected her satisfaction! She acknowledged she felt safe there and was looking forward to going again later that week.

It was interesting talking to a friend later in the week. He asked me about the male caregivers in our group. He told me he belonged to two different support groups. In each one the dynamics between the men and women, caregivers and loved ones, was unique to each group. Being a female caregiver, I definitely did not see from his perspective instinctively. But I wanted to learn and assured him I wanted to visit his support groups. Caregiving was opening my eyes to see the world from a broader perspective.

I remember watching one friend hand her husband his medication while we were out having lunch. She carried his pills and presented them to him as needed. I observed and learned that was an option. On other occasions, caregivers buttered bagels or fixed tea for their loved ones. Thinking and doing for two all the time was a new concept for me.

I learned that partners had to help each other, even in public, do many things that they might otherwise not have done in former situations. We learned from each other, we accepted each other, we supported each other and enjoyed our exchanges in a social setting.

"See you next Wednesday! Thank you for being my friend!" was the farewell each week.

And on the way home loved ones remarked, as reported each week, "I like those people. I hope we will see them again."

Interesting, loved ones each had similar comments. For those with Alzheimer's disease it was like meeting new friends, week after week. We all kept Wednesdays open for our coffee gathering or for attending other Alzheimer Society-related activities. We acknowledged it was good to be able to share what we had learned and done to get through our week, to learn what we might expect down the road, especially to get ready for what might be ahead. After all, each one of us was headed in the same direction, just momentarily on different points along the spectrum.

Our lifeline friends were originally from four different countries, currently living in two different towns, with personal histories from different walks of life. In our diverse group we had three who had been teachers, one librarian and writer, one committed housewife and mother, and another, a dental assistant. Three had been in marketing, and at least three had owned businesses. One had a military and business management background, while one was a professional musician, one a hobby musician, and another a website designer. All in our group had raised families as parents, a good practice for being a caregiver. Evolving experts at caring.

We were about the same age, somewhere in our seventies and early eighties, but our life experiences varied greatly. Most had traveled extensively, most had lived in places other than where we were now. Most had been on some type of cruise. Some were more active than others. Email came easy to some, while others preferred the phone. But the mix worked. Maybe it was that diversity that kept us together, or perhaps it was that our loved ones had slightly different variations of dementia and so we could learn from each other as one progressed ahead of another. Maybe it was the knowing how important it was to have our cherished lifelines. Or maybe it was that we each enjoyed being part of a group of truly caring people who wanted to help each other through the unfamiliar territory of memory loss. We were living proof that lifelines were so important.

Whatever the reasons, I, for one, was grateful to have shared many Wednesdays with those who became our friends . . . over and over again!

The Andrew Gold song from 1978, "Thank You for Being A Friend," took on a meaning of great significance as years went by.

20 EXPRESS AND CREATE

"What do you think about this picture?" the art therapist asked. "How does it make you feel?"

That was all she said as she smiled and pointed to the image projected on the large monitor hanging on the wall. And then she waited. The class members looked at the painting and thought about the question. That week the wall monitor was displaying a colorful painting, *Nocturnal Festivity*, by a Swiss-German artist, Paul Klee.

Klee was known not only as a father of abstract art but a leader of many twentieth century art movements. But it did not matter that only a couple members knew Klee's name or his works. The six pictures chosen for observation that day generated much discussion among the seniors as they deliberated characteristics they saw in each one.

"I like the colors," My Love answered when it was his turn. And then he added, "Look at his lines. He draws with such sharp, defined lines." Without realizing it, he had noticed Klee's connection to architecture.

"Look how the colors seem to play together," another observed. He picked up on an important characteristic. I had learned in college that Klee loved the magic of color.

I was always amazed at the genuine thought the members of that class gave when they answered. Few, if any, had an art background. Most were there for some group time and friendships and the secure social atmosphere the class offered, rarely to learn about art. Sometimes I felt those with memory loss seemed more discerning and less distracted in their comments than those of us with cluttered memories.

My Love and I had been in that class for more than four years. We had met many people who loved participating as much as we did. Comprised of caregivers, each with their loved one, the express and create class was a favorite. My Love knew when Monday came it was time to go to class.

It seemed that as his memory diminished, he still was able to convey thoughts through his projects. Watercolor, chalks, string, pencils, acrylics, the media, the process, it did not matter. His ability to focus on his work was evident. His love for art was displayed each week as he produced masterpiece after masterpiece! It would have been a devastating day if he had to miss the express and create class. My job was to be sure he was there!

The atmosphere in the class, by design, provided a safe place to discuss without judgment. Those in the class had learned, after only one meeting, that they could express their opinions without being right or wrong. It didn't take long to learn that members were not judged for their comments, that one belief was as important as another.

Very important to the comfort, safety, and day-to-day basic living, especially for one with memory loss, was a truly benign setting. With a background of trust and the lack of fear, the brain seemed to find memories more readily in that class. Most times at the end of an express and create session, the feelings we all left with were positive. Many could have stayed longer just to experience the acceptance one felt.

"It looks like Christmas Eve!" another continued evaluating the painting on the monitor screen. "Look at all those lights!"

"I think it feels very warm," another member quietly added. "Like a summer night. It must be somewhere where Christmas is warm, then, eh? Maybe in the Caribbean?" He chuckled.

"Do you like the painting?" asked the therapist.

"I do," answered the member, without adding anything more.

"All the pictures we looked at today look like he scratched them somehow. Look at the sharp, contrasting lines," came a comment with a different perspective.

"They do look scratched, don't they?" the therapist remarked. "After the break we will do a little scratching ourselves. Let's have coffee and come back to do our project."

I held back as the class members went to the kitchen. Noticing one caregiver seemed a little down, I waited for her. She mentioned she had been having such a hard morning with her spouse. He kept forgetting he couldn't drive anymore, and he was fighting with her because he wanted to drive to class.

"But do you see how he has abandoned his desire to drive when he gets here? He just wants to talk about the paintings we look at," she said, amazed at what she was witnessing.

"It must make you feel much better, too!" I said to her, noticing she seemed calmer now than when the two of them arrived only one hour before.

"Yes, I always look forward to this class. I get as much from it as he does! Maybe more. Such a great distraction for a short period in our day. I am so grateful."

I could not have agreed with her more! Besides, that was how it was designed to work.

Being a caregiver for one with memory loss was stressful, at best, and could become quite debilitating for a caregiver, at worst, depending on how the disease and their relationship were progressing daily, or even just depending on the time of day.

In addition, when the caregiver was having personal medical issues, everyday-experiences brought challenging situations beyond what might be normal, adding to the anxiety of the relationship and ongoing situation.

It appeared to me that this couple had found the express and create program provided a way for the one with memory loss to have a creative outlet, a place to express himself, and sometimes even to act out without disapproval or judgment from the members in the program. At the same time, the caregiver received encouragement, guidance, and moments of recharging for the days, months, and sometimes years ahead. Perfect relief for both. Express and create.

After the break, the members were back in their seats, being asked to select their black scratch paper, either with silver, gold, or colors to show through the scratching. While everyone was drinking coffee, volunteers had placed skewers on the table, which would be used to scratch the papers.

And then the therapist turned on the music. The soothing therapeutic combination of art and music once again provided a relaxed environment for uninterrupted safety and freedom.

Watching each person begin to focus on their own work was evidence to me of how safe they felt in the room with twelve other people they had only met in that class. I was witnessing how the social atmosphere had bred friendly relationships and a sense of trust that enabled each one to create freely, sharing whatever was on their mind.

My Love's picture that day was intriguing to me. He had chosen to scratch black-on-silver paper, where the silver came through when he scratched away the black. He decided to add color pastels over top of some black areas merely because he liked color—how appropriate for a Klee study. His picture did seem to capture the essence of *Nocturnal Festivity.*

Each member's picture revealed ideas or thoughts they had kept inside that they now felt free to release. Not all scratched pictures mirrored paintings of Paul Klee. One loved one had created shapes with color coming through the black. Another had straight lines of gold showing through black. I had watched one member spend lots of time removing every spec of black, revealing lots of colors. All so different!

We framed My Love's scratch picture, so it could join the other paintings we had put on his gallery wall in our home. I loved to look at his pictures and remember watching him create each one. I remembered how immersed in a technique or process he would become, thinking only of his project. That class had been far more about being an intervention than art. So fortunate.

When Monday came, if he were having an anxiety attack, I never knew whether to grab him and get him in the car or not. If I could get him seated in the classroom, he would be fine. It seemed he always left his anxiety, his Alzheimer's disease, and COPD somewhere else for the rest of the day. It reminded me of his former three-month intervention, when he painted each day and had almost no anxiety attacks.

We had been in that class over four years, during which time his throat or chest rarely hurt, he never had an anxiety attack, and he seldom coughed. He didn't need his inhalers. His mind was entirely focused. I even thought his Alzheimer's disease was on hold while he was in his zone, doing his artwork, without any other thoughts.

My Love was a perfect example of what that class could do for someone with Alzheimer's disease accompanied by anxiety. I believed that was what it was created to do!

The express and create class had been a perfect intervention for My Love.

Before we left class each week, the therapist had each person show what they had done. When members revealed their finished work, rarely were there duplications. The results showed a vast range of interests. And the compliments each one received from their classmates were worth coming to class to hear. Each one went home feeling they had value as a person and a place to be recognized, encouraged, and accepted by others in the room. If only life outside our bubble could be that way!

I truly felt that class, sponsored by the Alzheimer Society in our area, might be duplicated in other areas with the right leader. I often wondered if it could work as an intervention for any caregiver-loved one relationship where other intense diseases were impacting lives. It was such a positive place for couples who otherwise might have been home arguing about who could or could not drive. Instead, as promised, this class provided perfect social experiences and cultivated friendships in a safe atmosphere.

Many participants returned to be part of a second and third session of classes. Caregivers realized that class provided a beautiful way to give their loved ones an enjoyable social experience while the caregivers themselves relaxed and enjoyed the needed socialization.

21 ART IN THE DARK

"Is it Monday? Are we going to our art class today?"

Art class, we incorrectly called it. The therapist had called it a place to "keep art in mind" while we created.

My Love had dementia and loved to go to class with others he had met through the Alzheimer Society-sponsored programs. The thought of going to our express and create session, a place to express ourselves through visual art making, always energized both of us. That class was where we spent the best hours in any week.

That morning was the first of a new series, the first class we had been to in several weeks since the previous session ended before the winter holiday. We had missed our Monday morning art group! Having supplies at home to work with was just not the same; plus, My Love found his zone in the positive social atmosphere that class provided.

Cautiously, I made a point not to get too excited while making breakfast. I did not want My Love to start one of his anxiety episodes, which would keep us home. I loved the class as much as he did. So, I kept the energy level low and hoped I would not do anything to trigger change.

We had no idea what activated his episodes, but if doctors called them anxiety related, surely the body must be responding to some unease. So, I intended to keep the status quo at equilibrium, helping life roll on smoothly. Whatever the reason, my rationale and efforts worked this time.

We put our boots and coats on, sent the dog to go to her kennel, went out, and locked the door behind us. Whew! Now to get to the car, through the snowy streets and the falling snow, to the parking lot in time for our class, before another episode began to rumble in My Love's chest. We did it.

In their office, we saw the familiar faces of the Society staff, all smiles, sharing hugs with good wishes for the new year. In the classroom were new couples ready for the class. One of the joys each session was meeting new people. We loved the art therapist who facilitated and guided us each week. She was the perfect person for such an occupation. Her personality brought smiles and laughter into the classroom.

The therapist's beautiful nature, her true caring and attentiveness, seemed to rub off on those in the room. Caregivers and loved ones alike might come to the class a bit down from being caught up in weekly memory loss cycles, but once in her classroom, many of those down spirits seemed to dissipate, if just for that short period. Our classes seemed to expand into an energy of love, shared among us all.

Time spent with this program always seemed to feed my soul, regenerate my caring spirit, and restore my nurturing skills so I could make it one more week as a caregiver. And for My Love, dodging an episode for a morning was worth being there. That was the point, to benefit both the caregiver and the loved one.

I looked forward to the class as much as My Love did. He was the person with dementia; I was the caregiver. But we were both able to be there because he had memory loss. We both benefited greatly from participation. Grateful.

Once settled in our seats, coffee in hand, we began the routine procedure of the class, discussing art created by established artists. That day we were talking about artist trading cards, with the intention that we would produce our own in the second hour of the class. And then we would exchange them among ourselves.

As I understood it, the idea of displaying art on small cards was started by a Swiss artist in

1997. During a convention, a Canadian artist noted that adults were trading sports cards, he picked up their idea, combined it with what he knew of small artist cards, and made a few changes. In 1997, artist trading cards showed up at the Alberta College of Art and Design in Calgary, Alberta.

This modification to the concept incorporated a trade-only practice. With his no-selling variation, he added the face-to-face element. Thus began a tradition. Thousands of artist trading cards have been traded among artists worldwide since 1997, many stored in albums, in the same plastic covers that sports fans used for protecting their sports cards. Wikipedia reported that in 2016 there were regular artist trading card sessions in thirty cities in the U.S., Canada, Australia, and Europe.

In our class, we talked about different media used on the cards we observed in photos. We discussed different possible themes we might use, made suggestions of what we liked, and even related to how small the cards were for details some artists had been able to produce.

And then the lights went out. It was nearly pitch black in the classroom. It was dark in the entire building, on the street, and throughout the neighborhood. Ice somewhere had snapped a line, or heavy snow had brought down the wires. We only knew for sure that we could see the glow from the Exit sign in the hallway. Windows to the grey skies were in the front offices. We were in the back, in the dark.

We laughed. It seemed the event brought ten strangers together quickly, bound by darkness. It was a crazy way to start our first class of the session. No one had any idea how long that darkness would last. Staff brought large emergency flashlights and placed them on the floor, shining the light on the ceiling to reflect into the room. Our eyes adjusted and, strangely, we all sat there, continuing our interest in the art trading card class. No one left. No one wanted to leave.

The trading cards were to be business card size and we needed light to see what we were doing on something so small. In the dark, we couldn't see to create them. So, what could we do instead?

The Universe always took care of things in my life. I just happened to have some black paper in my bag with me that day and offered it for use. Black paper in the dark! We wouldn't make trading cards, but it might be fun to work in the dark. I removed the paper from my bag and asked if we could use it. No one objected, so we went for it.

Our therapist handed out the paper; our volunteer passed the chalks around. We couldn't tell what colors we picked, we just grabbed a couple of chalk sticks and began to make marks on the paper, in the dark.

Those with cell phones turned on their flashlights now and again to check the marks on their paper. But it turned out to be fun, a new experience, to draw by feel of the chalk, by mentally remembering. We were all in the dark, drawing mystery pictures.

In this, our first express and create class of the new session, a couple attending expressed their reticence at producing art. They kept saying they weren't artists. Of course, we (those who had been in the class before) believed all of us were artists, some just waiting to be discovered! But this was not the time or class for that intellectual discussion!

Without heat, the room began to get cold. Quickly, we finished up making our marks on the black paper without knowing what we had drawn for sure, or where the colors had landed, or how our pages looked. Apparently, we didn't care.

However, even in the dark, before our time was over, everyone was involved, realizing there would be no judging of anyone's work, no right or wrong ideas on the paper, just appreciation of being with the others. Everyone realized that whatever we put on the paper was ok.

No one noticed who had Alzheimer's disease and who didn't. No one paid attention to who was a caregiver and who was a loved one. No one cared who drew what. We were just working on a project, using artist materials. This project seemed to bring those outliers into the fold, so they could also enjoy the fun of being there with us on our adventure doing art in the dark.

Before the following week, the therapist was going to spray the pages so that they wouldn't smear. Under the light from the fluorescents, we would see what we had drawn. We were going to have our own reveal at the start of the next class. And then we would make our trading cards.

Our art in the dark class was an unintended icebreaker!

And My Love never had an inkling of an episode arise the entire time we were in the dark, as if no episode and no memory loss would interrupt his perfect moments! Once again, I felt like he was in his element.

22 ART GALLERY TOUR

"Are we going to art soon?" My Love asked with great anticipation in his voice and sparkle in his eyes.

Magic happened just knowing we'd go to art on Monday morning.

I don't know what he would have done if I had said we couldn't go. I don't know what I would have done if I had to tell him he couldn't go!

My Love waited a week for that one hour he got to paint in a class. Painting on paper, cardboard, plaster, clay, or papier mâché. Watercolour painting, acrylic painting. Drawing with pencils, chalks, and pastels. He drew and painted trees. Pine trees. Rivers. Lakes. Pine trees. Trees.

He loved making cut-outs from colored paper, then recreating a new shape by combining them. He threaded string on broken twigs and a Viking ship magically appeared! He kept his focus when forming three-dimensional shapes and busts from blocks of clay. He made a bust of himself! My Love lived in his own world in that class.

We did weavings with various materials, we printed pictures using Styrofoam shapes, and we took prints off large soap bubbles blown with straws—all simple process projects that My Love usually took to another level when he added his imagination. That class was the distraction I prayed might intervene in his daily anxiety attacks, because it worked.

"You have aroused My Love's inner artist! It is the one thing we do during the week when he doesn't fight me or find excuses not to go. He loves it," I assured the art therapist.

Was My Love becoming a Grandpa Moses at seventy-eight? After all, Grandma Moses, the real one, Anna Mary Robertson Moses, started her new career painting folk art when she was seventy-eight! It didn't matter; he had awakened a dormant passion. But it appeared to be a passion that only blossomed in social settings, especially our express and create class.

We had cleared one wall in our home so it could become My Love's own gallery wall. His framed paintings brought so much warmth and happiness to the room. I loved having them as part of the décor. His other projects adorned shelves and other wall spaces. I loved hearing him laugh or speak of them when he reflected on making them. His intensity and his focus had been a treat for me to witness and remember.

One of his favourite projects had been making masks during the week of Halloween. We painted on blank pre-made masks. No topic was assigned. After studying masks of the world for the first hour, our second hour was spent decorating our own.

We could paint whatever we wanted on our own mask. His mask looked like Charlie Chaplin to me. Of course, he no longer knew who that was.

"Just a face," he told me.

He photographed the two of us, head-by-head, he, Charlie Chaplin, and me, covered by my Geisha girl flowered face.

That picture sat framed on a nearby table. I laughed hearing him laugh every time he looked at the two of us. Another layer of happy results from our class!

~

On the last scheduled day of the express and create classes, the therapist arranged for us to attend the current show at the local art gallery, where we would be toured through what was on display.

The gallery was a wonderful art facility for any town, offering membership in guilds. Their facilities housed studios dedicated to photography, hand-weaving, spinning, sculpture, woodcarving, ceramics, fine arts, pottery, fibre arts, and hooking craft.

Normally, a tour of the open guild rooms was included. The woodshop workers loved to share and explain their carved and whittled pieces of various types of wood, including the canes they made with birds on top of the handles. In the weaving room, although no weavers were working, we saw finished work as well as evolving thread designs on various sized floor and hand looms. We shared a small demo loom, passing it around the table while we enjoyed cookies and tea. Anyone who wanted to could learn how a loom worked by using that small one!

During our two hours, some of those with memory loss drifted off from the group. Others got energized by the stimulation of the colour and objects being displayed throughout and acted out, as might be the case with a class of younger children in a place with such energy. Caregivers were on high alert.

My Love was one who was energized. He had art in his DNA. He loved to see art and to create it, and even handle it. I knew he did not see the "Please do not touch" signs placed among the artwork pieces, on the walls, in the halls, or in the pathway of the conservatory. Whether that was conscious or not, I cannot say anymore, for he always was a hands-on type of art inspector.

When I noticed he was overly curious, I tried to pull back his hands if they reached out, as if his child were still alive inside. And like a child, he resisted my interfering by pushing me away! Awkward!

Included at the end of the tour was a walk through a small, glass-covered conservatory where larger works of ceramic art had been permanently placed among thriving plants. Larger-than-life-size ceramic human figures representing wind, earth, fire, and water stood in appropriate locations in the gardens. Ceramic fish "floated" beside real carp swimming with colourful koi in a pond winding through the room.

We loved walking through the conservatory. The large statues of the four elements usually generated a comment about their height, unusual features, and abstracted companion accessories. One time My Love took his phone and photographed them in their stationary locations. He was fascinated with the pictures he had taken, spending hours looking at them later.

While walking through the gallery and conservatory, I loved the feeling of revitalization I got when taking in new art. My soul was bursting. I was sometimes even quite taken by the many plants in the conservatory and wandered ahead to see those growing in the nursery.

"Who is that?"

Not recognizing the voice, I turned around to see the curator standing in the doorway.

. Then I got a glimpse of My Love, who had stepped up into the exhibit. He was sporting a big bright smile as he stood with his arm around the shoulders of the ceramic representation of "Wind," who was just a few inches taller than My Love.

"My new friend!" he innocently proclaimed, standing tall, beaming ear-to-ear!

Oh my! I was horror struck! Taking big strides to get near him, I carefully, reached my hand out to him, hoping he would grab hold and I could lead him out of the exhibit. He ignored me.

So, as if I knew what I were doing, I stepped into the exhibit and took his hand as I would with a child. I quietly let him know this was not where guests of the gallery were supposed to walk. We were supposed to stay on the path. Without warning, I pulled him toward the path, whispering firmly, "You must come with me, now."

He heard me. He came.

I didn't know if this tour interruption would turn into a stand-off, or if I would have to enlist the help of our class members. The curator stood hovering; I felt like I was prey for a hawk! Hand in hand, we stepped down out of the display and back onto the path.

I realized I had relied on him to follow the rules. That was supposed to have been my job! So much for me to remember! I had left his side for a second. One second. I wanted to look at a miniature plant growing beside the path, just at the same moment he chose to step up into the exhibit.

We almost owned that statue! But "Wind" still stands in the conservatory and we are still welcome to visit.

 **23** INTERVENTION

"Your paints are in the art tub by your table. Would you like to paint?" I asked My Love. "You have lots of white paint." I was eager to rejuvenate his interest, to encourage activity at home.

My Love lacked a hobby since selling his boat several years earlier. He had the dog, and indeed, loved her. But I detected he'd benefit from another, more personal, pastime. I was hoping he'd find a reason to get off the couch and become self-motivated to rekindle his art interest, possibly without persuasion each time. It'd give him something to think about during the day. Purpose.

"No. It's ok," he told me. "I'll just paint in class."

Hmmm. A clue. What did art class offer that we did not have at home? Social. We had no people. I couldn't change that. Music. We could add music in the room. So, I turned on some John Barry music and let it play. I wanted to find a strategy that worked.

"That's nice," he let me know he approved. But music did not make him think about painting.

"We listen to that music in art class," I reminded him. I could see he was thinking about something. I just let the music play.

Then for some reason, one day I tumbled! My eyes opened. It became apparent to me that painting had been one thing he had been able to do that had not aroused his mystery anxiety disorder, had not stimulated any dementia characteristics, and had been void of any COPD indicators. He never had any symptoms while at express and create class nor following the class for a short period. He had no episodes surrounding his art making. Bingo! Maybe.

And then, synchronicity! During a session with my therapist, we watched a TED Talk given by Moshe Szyf, epigeneticist, and I heard him suggest that an intervention could interrupt stress. My doctor smiled. He knew I understood I needed to find an intervention for My Love's episode experiences, perhaps something other than the addictive anxiety medication. My mind clicked on.

My sister had bought us a small folding table the previous summer. I put the plastic storage tub of paints, canvases, pencils, and tablets of watercolor papers beside the table. And then, in plain sight, I placed a sheet of watercolor paper on the table beside the tubes of paint and brushes. All he had to do was to sit down and begin. I hoped I had created an invitation, a lure, for him to take up a hobby at home. Then, I waited.

Six months later, I was typing away and looked up. Yes, after six months, there he was, seated at the table, drawing a picture of Mypsy, our dog. I stopped typing. I tightened my lips. I didn't want to say a thing to ruin the scene. After lunch he spent nearly three hours painting his dog picture, listening to John Barry music providing a soft background to this moment.

Then the most amazing thing happened, or didn't, actually. His usual late afternoon anxiety time came. He had no episode. After dinner, he had no episode. I sat anticipating. Nothing. I cleared my thoughts. I did not want to jinx what was happening. But it seemed to me his intense focus on his artwork was in some way having the same effect on him as the breathing device had when he breathed. Distraction.

Did he now have two innocuous props he could use? It seemed the breathing and the painting were each acting to resist any oncoming anxiety. But it looked as if art time *prevented the pain from ever beginning*, better than the breathing device, which we activated after the anxiety arrived. Would something he loved perform as an intervention? Was it the intense concentration? Or the passion? Far better than that wee little pill!

The second day, I mentioned to him that maybe his creative time had successfully helped him dodge an episode. Somehow, he understood! Within a few minutes, he had chosen a picture to use as a guide to paint and was seated at the table picking out his colors. I wondered if he really comprehended what I had said.

Then, following the second afternoon of painting, again he had no episode. The evening was calm. He went to bed without anxiety. Two days in a row! Art and music had altered something. Blessings.

I knew we weren't out of the woods. I could not become complacent. Anxiety could find another exit route. I kept supporting what was working.

"I'm out of white paint," he mentioned out of the blue.

"Do you want more?" I asked. He immediately showed me he had none. I forgot watercolor normally had no white in the pallet. And he just wanted white! He was into his painting!

Without thinking twice, I obliged and drove to a nearby art store and returned with two full sets of colors, each with a white tube of paint! A single tube of white watercolor paint was not easy to find.

What if art and music would become a remedy that would solve his years-long chest pain and anxiety? I would be over the moon for him, and for me. I was watching his love-of-creating-art-with-music rescue My Love from his stress. Art and music therapy! Was it possible relief could be so simple? Was this truly an intervention, like Moshe Szyf had described. "If it's not broken, don't try to fix it" came to mind! Time for everyone to remind educators of the benefits for keeping art and music classes in the school curriculum. Seriously!

"Are you going to use the new paints we bought?" I asked, hoping he would sit and paint again for the third day. I wanted to confirm that his activities could hold off another anxiety episode. If only.

His response was firm. "When I want to paint, I will paint." He did not touch the brushes.

Oh, dear. Maybe, I was being too controlling. After all, he just was being an artist! I realized then that he didn't understand the calming value of his painting. Maybe I didn't get the hook strategy just right either! I would go back online to check. I backed off.

Day three. No painting, but no episode.

Day four, he painted. Bed time and again he was without his chest pain. Crossing my fingers, I was feeling hopeful! Maybe the strategy was working.

But, *nooooo*! There was that rumble sound, that clearing his throat, that harrumphing sound I hoped would have been averted. An episode came and lasted two hours that night. I tweaked the schedule and suggested he start painting earlier. I wanted to see if that tricky anxiety could be fooled into staying away if My Love began painting earlier. Another test. Another period of wait-and-see. We were getting closer, I was sure of it.

Again, our life changed. Every day I promised myself not to push any issue. I didn't lecture. I bit my tongue. I put out the watercolor paper and waited. He painted. Another good day!

~

My Love painted at home for about three months. When he painted, those days became a day without an episode. Without anxiety, he was much more relaxed. Our life was almost . . . close to some kind of normal. The intervention of art and music as therapy had worked.

And then other physical issues rose to intervene in his intervention! He painted a couple days in the hospital. But after he was sent home, even with the paints and brushes in clear view, waiting on the table, he did not paint at home again.

His hospital stay had changed him. There were so many things still going on with My Love's health.

We were fortunate to have found one intervention for a short time.

~

"Who's singing that?" My Love turned to ask me, while drinking his breakfast coffee.

He had a smile on his face. I knew he liked Emmy Lou Harris and Mark Knopfler's album, *All the Roadrunning*. We both loved their harmony and sweet sounds. I had picked it for our morning music.

"It's Mark Knopfler and Emmy Lou Harris. You like it?" I answered.

He smiled.

Music could set a tone in the room, so I played it quite often. I much preferred it to the negative reports on the news station My Love always seemed to find on the television as soon as he arrived in the living room. The familiar faces of the announcers seemed to increase his feeling of security. So, I asked him to pick the TV channel, but mute the sound while we listened to music from my laptop, my compromise. Generally, he would if he could still watch the screen. Feeling in charge of the TV remote was one freedom I did not need to take away from him. In time, his desire to choose stations would fade on its own. There were few shows I cared to watch anyway, so it was seldom an issue.

"Who is that singing?" My Love asked, not remembering he had asked only two minutes earlier.

"It is Mark Knopfler and Emmy Lou Harris. They're singing 'Beyond My Wildest Dreams.' You like it?" I asked.

"Kind of like us?" he said, smiling proudly. Had My Love had a moment of clarity? "And you're beyond my wildest dreams!" He grinned as he reached over to grab my hand. I loved when he had his moments of sweetness.

"But who is singing it?" he asked, again unaware he had just asked.

I could never presuppose anything. One second of time changed the world. I was just happy My Love was enjoying the music. It relaxed him and seemed to keep his anxiety attacks at bay. If he could get through any period of time without anxiety entering the picture, I felt we had been incredibly successful!

Morning and evening seemed to be the time periods his anxiety surfaced. As a warning, a breathlessness came over him and then I'd see him reach for the middle of his chest. He was going to have what doctors called an anxiety attack, even though not one had ever seen what he experienced.

But then, after more than two years of not knowing for sure, we happened to be in My Love's doctor's office when he began to have one of his attacks. I was elated. Someone besides me was going to be able to see what happened. His doctor verified, indeed, My Love was having an anxiety attack.

First My Love began to clear his throat, *harrumph, harrumph*, and then seemed to become overwhelmed, feeling he could not breathe. When he became breathless, he harrumphed, he coughed, held his chest. He always felt there was a physical blockage in his airway. But no phlegm came. His doctor finally watched what I had seen for a long time.

Early on, I had heard that getting more oxygen into his lungs might reduce his feeling of breathlessness and thus lessen the stress he was feeling and perhaps stop the attack. So, I continued to encourage breathing with his breathing device, the device for loosening phlegm through vibrations, phlegm he never had had. But it seemed to calm him and focus his breath during his anxious times.

"Who is singing that song?" he asked me not long after I had identified the previous singers. "Are they singing in the dining room?"

He heard where the sound was coming from but saw no one. I realized he thought Mark and Emmy Lou were physically singing in the dining room. I wish!

"No, the songs are on my phone."

I wished I could have drawn out that conversation. I could have stopped his anxiety. But it passed by so quickly, and he was coughing once again.

I was forever explaining that sounds did not always have someone real in the room. It sounded like the conversation we'd had about the "Birdsong" alarm coming from my phone in the morning. Maybe he liked having the TV on because the sound of voices made it seem like people on the screen were in the room.

Of course, one of my intentions playing the music was to provide a diversion, an intervention, to his morning attacks. He was a person of routine and I wondered if routine enhanced his attacks. When he heard the music, it was sometimes similar to painting, a new and unexpected activity he could focus on that calmed him. Many times, music and art seemed to prevent an episode.

Art and music . . . far better than little pills. I played music, hoping to use it to alter the morning schedule, interject a diversion, intervene into his brain patterns. I knew it was possible. He had succeeded before by painting. But that was before his second hospital stay and he never sat to paint at home again. Maybe there could be something else.

As long as I played favorite music at different times and kept canvas and paints on the table, there was always the chance he might sit down and paint. One of the senior daycare providers offered a good art program. My Love was on the waiting list. We had to wait three more months. In the meantime, I kept looking for a new intervention, one he would find as much joy in as much as he found in his art.

24 FANCY PANTS DANCER

Since the day I first met My Love, he had a rhythm in his gait. He had a bounce and energy that moved him effortlessly from step to step. He did not just walk. Sometimes, he'd almost skip, with an easy, loose pace. His long stride out-walked me every time. He seldom liked sitting still.

In much younger years, I probably would have asked him, "Do you have ants in your pants?"

Even now, I knew his aging body still needed to be active. He had been a skier and instructor. He liked to walk a lot. He was a swimmer and life-guard earlier in life. His body was designed to be in motion, outdoors if possible, in some manner, all the time. And he loved to dance. His whole body pranced about as he reveled in the pleasure his body was feeling. He seemed carefree and demonstrated that through his fancy footwork and expressive moves. When he danced, his eyes twinkled, his legs carried him all over the floor with the sounds of the music; he moved easily, he danced effortlessly. He swayed while his arms moved gracefully back and forth, side to side, following the rhythms and beat.

Even his hands got in the act as they grooved to the music. Undulation.

"You are such a Fancy Pants Dancer!" I'd say as he'd twirl me around and under, in front and in back, as he led me through dance after dance. Of course, he had slowed down a bit. But I still called him that. His whole body loved dancing, and despite our increasing limitations, I tried to keep up with his dance moves.

It did not matter whether Glen Miller's big band or Sinatra was the music source, he would twirl us around on the floor. If Elvis Presley were singing, My Love guided me slowly through a fast dance. He could twist with the best of them. When "The Great Pretender" by The Platters came on, we would slow dance, a nice close, slow dance. He'd hold me tight. Or if he heard Journey or the Eagles, he'd be up on his feet. Yes, he was a great dancer. He danced far better than I did, but he guided me with just a touch of his hand to my back, or a squeeze to my fingers. We had fun together. We always had fun.

When we began getting involved with the Alzheimer Society programs, we learned they sponsored dances. The first one we attended was their Valentine's Dance, "Waltz Down Memory Lane." It was another of their amazing programs, encouraging socialization for those with memory loss and their loved ones.

Seniors from several nearby homes for the aging came with their caregivers. Some arrived with canes. Some came with walkers, and some were in wheelchairs. Most everyone, nearly all those in attendance, danced in some manner, and all probably were home, exhausted, ready for bed by nine that night.

It brought tears to my eyes to see the grandchildren swaying hand in hand with their grandparents, to see young adults teaching new "steps" as they danced with a parent. I was always impressed by the youngest caregivers helping the oldest seniors to have a good time, two separated generations, joined by music and a social atmosphere.

And couples like My Love and me, who loved to dance, danced until we couldn't! I never thought about any one of the dancers having Alzheimer's disease. All any of them had was a big smile and a good time! For some, it was the best time of the year, maybe the best moment in their life.

Each year, My Love and I felt fortunate being there from the first note of the first song the DJ played. I loved hearing Bobby Darin singing "Mack the Knife," and any number of Elvis Presley songs, from "Love Me Tender" to "All Shook Up." The dance floor filled quickly when The Platters sang "Only You" or "My Prayer."

It was hard for everyone not to join in singing and dancing when the DJ played "Itsy Bitsy Teenie Weenie Yellow Polka Dot Bikini!" Had we been that crazy years ago? Happy, animated dancers rotated their bodies all around as Chubby Checker sang "The Twist."

"Girls just should not be doing those gyrations!" I could hear my father say, reminding me of my age as I watched the sparkling faces of those up and moving around. How happy they were.

By the time the Beach Boys began singing "I Get Around" very few were sitting in their seats. And those still seated were tapping their feet and bouncing their heads while they clapped their hands. Everyone was engaged in the party. The DJ started with music from the early 1950s and by the time the night was over he had gone through nearly seventy years of favorite songs. Music for everyone! Someone in the room always seemed to know the words to the songs he was playing. What a super evening! The small stories he told about various singers and their songs made them more interesting. Entertainment with our music.

My Love and I found the dance floor. We danced. We rested. We danced. He twirled. We cuddled. We traded partners. We danced. I rested. My Love danced while I rested. My Love went non-stop! I will forever have such heartwarming memories of our dancing!

There were spot dance prizes and door prizes. There were prizes for stopping closest to the far post or ending a dance under certain lights. Prizes were given for limbo winners, and the couple seeming to be Most in Love! One of the last awards of the evening was for Smooth Male Dancer. I was not surprised when they pointed to that "guy over there." I knew who they meant. "Twinkle-toes" was the name given to him by our Lifeliner friend who had been dancing with him at that moment. My Love had won a prize for his dancing that night! His love for dancing never ended. He did not need his memory to dance, to move around the floor. It was in his DNA and came naturally to him.

~

A year or so later we went to a jazz concert, also sponsored by the Alzheimer Society. The young group played many big band numbers. Most of the audience kept time to the music while making *I-want-to-get-up-and-dance* moves in their chairs. Some felt the beat of the bass as they tapped their fingers on the table. Others were bouncing their feet in time with the melodies. But no one was dancing on the big dance floor. Although it made no sense, I wondered if dancing was a no-no at senior music concerts.

It wasn't long before a pretty lady was roaming through the room, talking to guests at the tables, loosely swaying back and forth; obviously the music moved her!

"Doesn't this great music make you want to dance?"

She smiled, scanning through those seated at the tables, hoping to make eye contact with a potential dance partner. A lovely young lady, she was the coordinator for one of the senior homes who had brought a small group of residents to the concert. Many guests were not able to get up to dance, but even so, they smiled as they sat enjoying the songs from their own era, singing songs they remembered. But My Love loved to dance. He took the bait. He couldn't wait to get out onto the dance floor.

"Ah, someone has feet itching to dance!" the lady said as she saw My Love raise his hand and glance back at her.

He was up on his feet the minute she got to our table, his arm reaching out for her hand. Ready to dance with his new partner, his legs and arms began to groove to the music, even as he almost skipped toward the dance floor. He could hardly wait to get off the carpet and onto the tiles.

The band seemed encouraged by someone dancing. Was the music getting louder? Did dancers on the floor energize them? I could tell there was a subtle shift in the atmosphere and people began moving to join My Love and his partner on the dance floor. The band played well-loved music and favorite jazz songs few bands play today. They featured young singers imitating Dinah Washington, who sang with Woody Herman, or Helen O'Connell, who sang with Jimmy Dorsey. And one young man took on the character and voice of Frank Sinatra. I kept wanting one to imitate Molly Johnson, Canada's popular jazz vocalist, who even was known to speak in the rhythms of jazz.

The music the band chose was perfect for dancing—My Love's style of dancing. He just liked to move. And his new partner liked to dance. The fun they were having was contagious and started a trend. Others felt the beat, too. The dance floor was getting crowded! I was not able to dance because of hip pain at the time, but I was able to do that chair-dance thing and loved watching others enjoying the music. I knew My Love was happy at that moment. I believed My Love's soul barometer was reflecting his movements, indicating he was feeling good, tuned-in to the music and turned-on to dance.

No Alzheimer's disease, no COPD, no anxiety attack could slow down my Fancy Pants Dancer!

~

Fast forward three years. Health changed. Energy levels changed, his and mine. Fluctuating personality dynamics kept me on my toes. Life activities and physical weakness changed our focus. Whether we were ready or not, aging and illness kept us moving along the spectrums and, along the way, we endeavored to keep our lives as normal as possible.

Is there such a thing as normal, anywhere?

Finally, the evening of the Memory Lane Valentine's Dance came again. It was still a favorite dance, attended by many caregivers and loved ones alike. Once more, we looked forward to our first fun outing of the new year, in the early part of February!

Every year new couples arrived to hear their favorite songs. Through the night the sounds of the later decades were played until the DJ reached the music from the current years.

Each year we witnessed how the music, especially favorites of an era, brought would-be dancers with memory loss to life; how seniors with reduced abilities were still able to smile and, in some cases, sing words to favorite songs. None of that had changed. We were not disappointed. Music made people come alive.

But My Love had changed.

In three years, his memory had diminished. He still was a good actor at covering up what he did not remember, which meant he must have known he did not remember, but he couldn't recall whatever it was. He seldom admitted it. One day that acting ability would disappear and, for certain, he would lose many of his memories. I hoped we'd go to many more dances before then.

That third year, my Fancy Pants Dancer looked at me after only one dance.

"It hurts to breathe," he said, touching that familiar spot in the middle of his chest in a relaxed manner so as not to bring attention to his movements.

"Do we need to sit down?" I asked, unaware he was having trouble since he did not appear out of breath.

"No, it just hurts to breathe," he said again. "We can slow dance, but I don't want to fast dance tonight."

I was following his lead, this unfamiliar behavior on the dance floor caught me off guard. I had not been prepared to hear his outright admission. It was not like him. One more comment had taken me by surprise.

"You tell me what you want to do."

What else could I say? I could not feel what his pain felt like to him. I did not know how intense his discomfort was. He took me by the hand, twirled once, and led me back to the table. Ok. That was going to work. When he needed a rest, he would rest. I did not want to embarrass him. He had to be the one to control the dancing. He had a reputation to uphold!

I checked in with him, "Are you ok? Do we need to go get your Aerobika breather from your coat?"

I was so glad I had thought to bring it!

"No, I just need to sit here," he said, looking off toward the food table. "Is that alcohol-free punch?"

I went to look. The sign said, "Alcohol-free Fruit Juice." I nodded. He was thirsty. I brought two glasses back to the table.

Throughout the night My Love was in control of when we danced. When he chose to sit, we joined our Lifeliner Group at our special table. I would sometimes venture off to say hello to friends seated at other tables. When he stood up, I took that as a sign he wanted to dance and returned to his side. He was very tuned in to his breathing. I had never seen that before at any event. He sat out more dances than he ever had since I had known him.

My Fancy Pants Dancer was slowing down!

25 MORNING ALARM

"Chirp. Chirpy. Chirp."

I could barely hear it. But there it was again . . . my morning wake-up alarm coming from my cell phone out in the living room. I loved the sounds of small birds twittering as they awakened in a wooded area. The alarm played "Birdsong" from my iPhone at 6:50 each morning, whether I was awake or not. Far better than some loud buzzer blasting at me!

I charged my phone nightly by the couch; it was set on loud for me to hear it ringing from the back bedroom, although many mornings I slept right through all the sounds, anyway.

Whether I was waking or asleep, the program still played. If My Love was out in the living room, he heard it and let it play. It seemed a bit like being in the country.

The birds singing their birdy morning greetings were scheduled to play at first for one minute. Then the alarm rested and cycled around again. I need to find those settings. That wake-up music had been playing each morning for months.

That morning My Love and I both happened to be awake in the living room when it started to play.

"What is that?" he asked.

"The birds?" I asked. "They're my wake-up alarm." I went on, not realizing he was more than a little curious.

Thinking I'd made a joke, he asked, "No, really, what is it?"

"Really. It's my phone, an alarm in my phone," I said. "It's birds waking me up."

Puzzled, he asked me, "But, where are they, really? Are they actually in your phone?"

"Yes," I said, "coming from my phone."

"The birds are in your phone?" he asked again. "They sound like they are behind the couch." I heard him whisper to our dog, "Mypsy, she has ghosts in her phone!"

I wondered if he thought I was hiding real birds behind the couch or in my phone. I did not realize until then that he was serious. I began to wonder if this was how hallucinations in dementia began. Obviously, he was confused.

"No, where are they, really?" My Love asked again, beginning to get agitated.

I could tell he thought I was teasing him somehow.

I tried to explain. "The sound of the birds is like music in the phone. Someone recorded birds singing in the morning, just like someone recorded a singer for a CD. And then, in the same way, we listen to that singer through the phone, we listen to the recording of chirping birds coming from the phone."

That was very complicated! I was beginning to wonder how I could describe such a technical marvel in simpler terms. My turn for confusion.

But then, surprise! He seemed satisfied. "Oh, that's what it is." And he was done with the subject.

I am not sure he understood my explanation, but it did not matter because his mind had moved on. But I was surprised how long it took for me to find the simplest words to convey that the phone was playing a recording! Technology would have to remain among those things we took for granted and a topic I could not always explain!

It wasn't long before he had more trouble finding words. He would begin to ask for something, ". . . the pusher, the water . . ." and he would stop. "Oh, you know!" he would say, shaking his head, hoping I would figure out the word he was searching for, *TV remote*. "You know, what I use for bedtime."

No, I didn't know. It took great genius, far more than I could muster, to connect some of the unrelated words to the meanings he was searching for. I listened. I tried to sense his needs, missing the mark often.

When his words would not come, he began to find other ways to relate. Waving his arms, shifting his eyes, or moving his head helped him express even though he was silent. His need to communicate struggled onward. I observed, desperately trying to put myself in his shoes.

"You mean the dog wants out?" I'd ask.

His face would relax, and he'd smile. I got it! He had used his eyes to show me the door. His brain was not making connections. Each day I was being tested. A big hug went a long way to prove that I was there and knew his agony. His cuddle in return showed me he was glad I was trying to understand him. It became scary when he began to wonder who the one cuddling him was. I held on.

"Are you coming from the kitchen? Bring me some . . ." And he stopped.

I couldn't guess what he wanted. He had to tell me somehow. So, he shook his hands over his food.

"Ah, you want salt and pepper?" I asked, thinking I had figured it out.

"No." He shook his hand again. "Red. You know. Red."

I didn't know. I was stuck on salt and pepper. What other way could he tell me what a "red" shaker meant? If I had not been going to the fridge at the time, I would not have recognized that he wanted ketchup. I saw the bottle. *Red*! I fluked that one!

"You want ketchup?" I asked.

He took a deep breath, smiled, and shook his head yes.

Words! Understanding. Confusion. He was having trouble getting words to come to the surface when he needed them. So many words and meanings had already been forgotten. At least it seemed if I were patient and focused, I might be able to sense his emotions surrounding the forgotten words. He could still be connected to our world.

 **26** HELLO. HELLO?

One day, while in the food store, in line to check out, my cell phone began to ring.

Brinnng-da, brinnng-da

I reached into my purse to grab and quickly silence it. In my haste, I did not look at the caller's name before answering.

"Hello . . ."

No answer.

All I heard was, "Harrumph, harrumph."

"My Love, is that you? Are you ok?"

I immediately recognized My Love's COPD cough and throat clearing that had been ongoing for a couple of years. At that point in his Alzheimer's disease, I was able to leave My Love alone with the dog for two or three hours at a time. And at that time, he was able to use his cell phone to call me if he needed me, which was not often at first. But I felt he'd be ok.

Again, I heard, "Harrumph, harrumph."

"My Love, is that you?" once more I asked for a response.

"Harrumph, harrumph, harrumph . . ."

"My Love, do I need to come home?"

"Harrumph, harrumph."

Each time before I left, I evaluated the situation. At that point in time, short errands still seemed quite feasible on a typical day. He didn't want to go along at first. Longer trips, an hour away, were still workable for one-hour appointments if I called him a couple of times. He never wanted to go with me. His iPad and phone-camera could occupy him while I was away. But because our life seemed to happen to us in surprises, I always tried to call. Now he was calling me.

But this time, I could hear no words. Only the continued throat clearing. To me, standing blocks away in a store, it seemed like My Love's responses, his sounds, were telling me to leave the store and come home.

I believed his noises were in response to my questions. Maybe he was having a hard time breathing. Maybe he had fallen and was unable to move or speak. I knew he no longer knew how to call 911, even though it was on his cell phone speed dial. In fact, I was surprised he had been able to think clearly enough to dial me using his phone!

For one with Alzheimer's disease, struggling with those simple tasks would be normal.

I spoke into the phone, "Ok, I'm coming home right now."

I kept my ear to the phone. I could only hope My Love heard and realized that I understood he was having problems breathing and I was on my way home at that moment. What else could I do?

Moving quickly, I turned my phone onto "speaker" and dropped it inside my purse, leaving it turned on. I put my basket of goodies off to the side; the ice cream, the detergent, the veggies. Sorry. I didn't have time to wait in a lineup to explain. Someone else would have to put the goods back on the shelves. I reached into the depth of my open purse, grabbed my car keys, and made a swift exit to the parking lot and my car.

After practically diving into the driver's seat, I put my phone in the console cup by my side, hoping I could hear more. No more coughing. No more noise. Nothing. What speed limit? I am sure I got home in under four minutes . . . just a few blocks!

Luckily the elevator came quickly, and I was the only one on for the ride up to our floor. As I grabbed the apartment door handle, I realized it was unlocked. I opened it and anxiously stepped inside.

I could see right away my love was sitting outside on the balcony. Really? He was sitting casually outside on the balcony! He looked up from playing with the dog and smiled and lifted his hand, acknowledging that I was home.

Out of breath from my quick run-walk down the hall, I got to the balcony door and asked, "Are you ok now?"

It was apparent he wondered at my bizarre question insinuating something might be wrong.

"I'm ok. Why?" My Love had a puzzled look on his face.

Looking around for his phone, I said, "You just called me, but you could not talk!"

He was confused. I was confused. I am not sure he could tell me what was going on. Dang it! I was annoyed, and it was coming out in my voice. Of course, I was glad he was fine, but at the same time, I was annoyed that I had gone through all the rush and urgency . . . and he was *fine*!

Finally, he spoke, "I never called you."

He had a very defensive tone, my clue he really did not phone me, and further, he did not know he phoned me. His phone must have made a pocket dialed call or maybe he hit a button without realizing it, which made the call. Who knows why? He played with his phone quite a bit. It only sent and received calls, but he loved using the camera; it took wonderful pictures! Now we learned it also made phantom phone calls.

I glanced at his phone sitting over on the table beside him. Yep, we were still connected!

"You called me, yes, you called me. See on the phone, we have not hung up yet."

He had no idea what I was talking about.

I knew as the words left my mouth what had happened. I could hear the frustration in my voice. How terrible it must have made him feel; he truly did not know he had dialed me! He had no idea what all the fuss was about.

But when I heard no voice answer me over the phone and only his throat clearing, which just happened to coincide with the timing of my questions, I envisioned all sorts of things going wrong. How mixed up it became so quickly! My relief was coming out, even while knowing I was hoodwinked by a cell phone!

My Love insisted he never called me, and I believed him. I had to stop talking about it. His agitation was beginning. I had essentially accused him, and he had done nothing! I was so sorry I had gotten upset. But so quickly, My Love was annoyed with me and could not hear me say "sorry."

I just quietly turned off the call between us, which was still open on his phone. I hoped his Alzheimer's disease would bail me out, anticipating his forgetfulness would allow the frustration to dissipate. For me, I hoped I could learn to be kinder! What a blessing he forgot some of those moments where I lost my cool when I didn't take time to breathe. *I felt I was forgiven.*

And then I went back to the store to re-shop my list!

27 RED SURPRISE

Every day for the past few years, while blow drying my hair, I used the mirror in the back of my curio cabinet in the dining room to see what I was doing. Our fifty-year-old apartment building had a fifty-year-old electrical system with a wiring scheme that was not designed to accommodate "modern" appliances. I had screwed a power outlet into a light-socket over the bathroom sink. My make-shift plug would blow a fuse if I used a hairdryer. When I needed a mirror, the curio cabinet was perfect, and the power in the dining room worked.

For some reason, that day I was focused on a couple of standing items on the top shelf in that cabinet, two small hand-painted saucers, gifts from a dear friend over thirty years earlier. I was far away, remembering the Christmases when my friend had given each one to me. I noticed they were set off against a background of red, something I had never observed before. I refocused my vision, noticing the red area looked like an envelope. Up close I could see my name lightly written on it. What the heck was it? Why was it sitting inside my cabinet?

Ah, and I thought My Love had forgotten Valentine's Day, I said to myself.

He must have been kidding when he somewhat sadly told me he had forgotten it was Valentine's Day and had not gotten me a card.

How did he get out to get me a Valentine? He must have made one!

Nothing made sense. I had to stop overthinking.

So, curiosity prevailed. I reached in through the side door and carefully slid the envelope out past my small angel with the harp, past my mother's green glass bird paperweight, and lastly, behind a blue ceramic bowl, which my grandson had made in high school for me. My treasures.

In the light, I looked closer. It was a good-sized envelope, thick like all the perfect cards My Love had picked over the years. I put my thumb under the seal and opened it. Even when My Love's memory was better, he never had hidden a card from me. Had I discovered a hiding place?

Of course, I was getting used to his new trea-sure hunts. Finding the kitchen dishes became a game after My Love dried and put them away . . . somewhere. Finding the knives tucked in beside the plates, the glasses sometimes in the fridge. After he took the groceries from the shopping bags, I would have to think like he did, guessing where he had put the canned soups or light bulbs. I thought ice cream would be a simple thing to put away, but it seldom made it to the freezer, meaning I had to be sure it did not melt wherever it was tucked away. Finding the ballooned cans of soda in the freezer made me happy I found them before they exploded. Reminding him or getting upset with him (after a while I couldn't help myself) made no difference. Usually, I found everything. And I found this envelope in time for Valentine's Day!

He was out, taking trash down to the dumpster. I could not wait to share my discovery!

As I slipped the card from the envelope, I could see the red ribbon on the front, the red satin bow that held it like part of the wreath of green evergreens, edged in snow. As the image came further into view, I realized it was my Christmas card, the one we could never find the previous Christmas, not a Valentine at all! And then some paper money fell out onto the floor. I looked into that mirror every day; I don't know how I missed the bright red envelope that had been there all those months.

I recalled the day My Love realized he could not find the Christmas card he had for me. He had been very troubled that day. He was concerned because he had not only gotten me a card but had put money in it. We had looked everywhere for his red envelope. I remember his anxiety distinctly because he went in circles, from bedroom to living room to dining room to bedroom, looking for the card. Then, together, we looked through every room, but we never found it. I had not seen it and finally accepted it must have fallen into one of the bags of trash he took down to the bin each day.

But for over two months it sat waiting to be discovered right in plain sight!

The smile was big on his face when he saw the pretty red card. He thought it was a beautiful card. But he did not recognize it.

"Why is it a Christmas card?" he asked me.

He did not connect that it was the card he had put there for me to find. How his mind had changed in that short time. Sadly, he would not understand my little laugh nor the warm-fuzzy love I felt when I finally found his well-hidden treasure.

28 FIRE IN THE NIGHT

I heard the birds chirping, the same birds that sang to me early every morning from the alarm clock in my cell phone. Was I dreaming, or had we finally gotten to bed only a couple hours earlier?

Only one hour after we had gone to bed the night before, the blaring fire alarm had sounded. An annoying, harsh sound, repeating and repeating! The sound was deafening. No one could sleep through it, even with earplugs! But I might not have heard it if the dog had not been walking all over my stomach in a state of panic.

When, finally, I was awake, I did smell the smoke. I even heard the sirens of the approaching fire trucks, even louder than that infuriating fire alarm. When I heard My Love saying all those swear words, I was convinced it was real. He grumbled if he had to wake up before the rising sun! He rarely wanted to get up for any alarm. Instead, he'd rather let the noise go on with the pillow over his head. But a fire alarm? I had to get him up, pandemonium or not.

We got dressed, put the leash on the dog so she would not get away. Mypsy was in a panic from the piercing sounds and would never hear "come" if she got loose. Those alarms were so painful to animal ears!

I grabbed my heavy coat, my "for an emergency" bag and my purse. I made sure My Love had his shoes and jacket on and his phone and his puffer in his pocket, and that he was holding the dog on her leash. Then we joined the others in the stairwell walking down to the lobby and out to the front parking lot. My legs ached with each step toward the ground, but I had no choice.

We descended floor by floor, getting closer to the smell of smoke. One of the younger men just ahead of us opened a door and saw firefighters in the hall. He shook his head "yes," there was a fire. Half awake, we kept walking down. Seven, six, five. Eighteen steps down per floor. Eleven flights. One hundred and ninety-eight steps. By then My Love was holding Mypsy in his arms. Four. Three.

Those folks who had gotten to the bottom that November night were already standing outside, shivering in t-shirts, cuddling in their bathrobes or buttoning their winter coats, whatever they had grabbed. Some wore slippers. I saw some with flip-flops and even a couple with no shoes at all. I counted twelve firemen, and one firewoman, dressed in heavy

IS THERE ANY ICE CREAM?

boots and tan and yellow fire gear, rushing around with masks covering their faces. They were busy carrying axes and cutters and rolling fans through the hall. They were stretching out long cables and using their walky-talkies. We leaned against the wall in the lobby, out of their way, where we watched and listened.

I looked down for my phone. No phone. Silly me. Never mind, we weren't hooked up to their communications, anyway. But we could hear the muffled words coming through their little speakers.

"On the seventh floor."

"Can you be sure everyone is out?"

"Do you need keys?"

"Check the sixth and eighth floors."

"Do you need hose?"

They were routinely checking everything!

Rubbing my eyes, I realized I not only forgot my phone, but also my glasses. Why did I do that? I was lucky I could see a bit without them. I only hoped we'd be going back to the apartment and not somewhere else temporarily.

Note to self: *put a spare pair of glasses in our emergency bag*!

I was getting drowsy. It must have shown on my face. The superintendent ran to open his office and motioned for us to go inside, as he ran on to help someone else in the lobby. Being invited into a warm room was a bonus of being My Love's tired senior partner so late at night! Maybe I looked older without glasses.

About an hour later they came to tell us the elevators were working again, that those not living on floors five through nine could go back to their apartments. That was us! Dogs, cats, kennels, kids, young, old, sleepy men and women, we all rode back up, stuffed into two cars!

Ready to try bed again, I was in the bathroom getting a glass of water when there on the counter I saw my phone, sitting beside my glasses. Relief. It was hard learning to take it with me.

I heard My Love begin to cough. *Oh, no!* Was that the result of physical exertion from this event? He had not coughed downstairs. He had not even coughed before bed. I thought we had had an episode-free day. But now, nearly one-thirty in the morning, his body was starting another "I can't breathe" incident.

I saw My Love was already on the couch breathing with his breathing device. At least he still had memory enough to know what would help him.

I knew I would sleep on the couch while he breathed for the time it took to get rid of that middle-of-the-chest mystery pain. It seemed to help if I were in the room. I didn't always count or breathe in and out with him anymore. He had learned to do that himself, an amazing feat for one with memory loss. I dozed.

When he seemed somewhat calmer—excuse me, when his body seemed somewhat calmer, because he told me he was always calm—I asked if he wanted to put a little green pill under his tongue so he could go to bed. He refused, fearing it would fall out as he breathed through the device. The pill was very tiny. I did not fight him. I'd have to wake up to find it if he lost it. And we did not want the dog to find it first. Ok. We waited.

Soon I heard, "Can I stop breathing now?"

I opened my eyes. I had fallen asleep. I realized he had been breathing with his device for more than another hour. It was after three in the morning! I assured him he could stop whenever he wanted to. He stopped. He was exhausted. I am sure he had taken in more than enough oxygen to cure any anxiety attack.

"Can you take your little pill now, so you can sleep?" I asked.

Thankfully, he agreed.

I woke the dog, who was sleeping on my lap. I handed My Love that tiny magic pill and watched as he put it under his tongue. In a few minutes it had dissolved. As I finished turning out the lights, he was climbing into bed. I never heard him settle or pull the covers over himself. I never felt the dog snuggle into my side. I, too, was out!

So, when I heard the chirping birds coming from my cell phone in the morning at seven, I knew I had to get up. My Love was still sleeping. At eight o'clock I had to wake him, since we had to be at my ultrasound appointment before noon; I had to take him with me for my sanity. Plus, I needed to be sure he was ok after taking his pill not that long before!

So, there we were, two of the lucky ones to start another new day. I didn't have time to reflect on the night before. I had to be awake, ready for the day ahead.

29 SPECTRUM SLIDE

"Would you like me to go get the mail?" My Love asked.

"Please, yes," I answered. "Do you know where the key is?" I asked, prompting him that he would need it.

We had gotten our mail from a locked box down in the lobby of our building for the last four years. Before that, the mailman put our mail through a clanging metal slot in our door, a routine not practiced any longer. Frequently, My Love would get our mail; most times he went without issue.

Confidently, he let me know he remembered. "It's hanging on the hook. The purple one for my neck."

So far, so good!

"Where is the mailbox?" he asked.

Oops!

"In the lobby, turn right off the elevator," I answered, recognizing that his forgetting our mailbox location might mean he would not be able to pick up our mail any longer.

"How do I find it?" he asked in all innocence.

In that split second when he no longer remembered the location of the mailbox, I felt sure that a scattering of brain cells had withered. He was still sliding along the spectrum of that dreaded dementia disease. He assured me he knew where the box was, but he could not explain it.

So, it was typical that when he returned from his mail foray saying, "There is no mail," I wondered.

Later, I would take the key and check the box. That day I found mostly fliers. I couldn't say if the mailman was late and I happened to go at the right time or if My Love never found the right box and lock to match his key. I would never know.

I hated taking his freedoms away. He could still go to the lobby and back and not get lost. And he hadn't yet lost the mailbox key. I could get the mail. But it made me wonder how long it would be before he wouldn't know how to use the key to get inside the building from his dog walk. He was sliding on his dementia spectrum slope and things were changing quickly. It wasn't a month or two ago when he could tell me the number on the mailbox, even the position in the group of boxes. But that memory, too, was vanishing.

Soon after he returned from the mailbox, I heard rattling in the kitchen. I thought he might be looking for the hook to hang the key back up.

"Do you need help?" I asked.

"No, I am sorting the trash. The bag is full. I will take it down." He generally took thrash to the dumpster when our trash was overflowing. Many times, we filled two small bags, making the trip more manageable.

"Ok. Do you know where the keys are?" I asked as I always did, to be sure he could get back in the building and, if needed, into the apartment.

"Hanging on the hook behind the door. Two keys are on a white strap with the red Canadian flag."

Does he know red?

"Did you check if they are there?" I asked because I had noticed the lanyard was missing.

Quiet.

Then he appeared in the doorway. "I don't see them. Where are they?"

"I don't know. Let's look. Where did you look?" I responded.

What made me think he would remember?

"I've looked everywhere, but I can't find them!" He sounded like he thought I had accused him of losing the keys.

Sometimes, no matter how much I tried, I guess I didn't speak in the right tone or say the right words. But I went to help My Love look again for the keys. Yes, he would have used them last because I always used my own ring of keys.

Our apartment was not that big. We routinely looked in the same places, the bedroom, on top of his dresser, and on his desk. Next, I suggested we search his pants pockets from the previous day and the pockets in his jacket in case he had forgotten they were there. I heard him picking through his three or four jackets figuring which one he had worn. I just let him look, although I wondered if he remembered what he was looking for.

Nothing.

Good grief! If he truly lost those door keys, I would not be able to let him help me with tasks that included leaving the apartment alone. He had helped me with "his jobs" for years; I knew I would eventually feel the addition of his duties added to my daily grind. Was I ready for more?

Relieving frustration, I glanced out the window for a peaceful moment. As my eyes were adjusting to the distance, they crossed the room to the table beside My Love's seat on the couch. There, my view was interrupted by a speck of red on white sticking out of the Kleenex box. It was not a tissue.

"Did you look on your table? See the Kleenex box?" I pointed, a wee prompt. "That might be the key strap sticking out of the top opening of that box."

"How did it get there?" My Love asked. "I didn't put it there."

Who knew? He fiddled with everything, wires, pencils, tissues, his phone, his iPad, glasses, his puffer, pictures, remotes; he rearranged his table daily. And now keys, but it really did not matter, anyway.

The key holder and keys were not part of his table, so because they were unfamiliar, and he did not know where they went, or maybe even what they were, he put them away, out of sight. I had seen that response to "not knowing" before. He just got rid of the unknown. But finding the door keys meant My Love could take the trash down one more time.

It seemed we spent time every day going through a form of hide-and-seek for some lost object, for his puffer, for his pajamas, for his little Kleenex packages, for the keys, for his water glass, even for a Christmas card one time. The same things always seemed to go missing.

He was his own organizer. My Love liked to be in charge. He tried to put things where he had before, only he couldn't, because he didn't remember where that was. Instead, he made up new places for them to be. It became normal to shake my head silently and begin our search route for whatever had been misplaced, or "relocated." Some things were never found.

Disappearances happened more often and would likely increase as time went forward. We looked for his asthma inhaler most often. I would take it, and he would take it back. He needed one in his pocket as a security blanket. And then it would disappear. And we would look. Sometimes two or three times a day! One time I found it in the fridge by the jam. Another time it was in the freezer, probably from when he was replenishing his ice cream! But it was truly an accidental find when it fell out of the toe of his shoe.

On the other hand, like organizing his side table, his memories seemed to retain his "how to do" activities. He loved helping me in the kitchen, drying dishes, setting up our dinner trays. I put away those don't-know-where-they-go things he left on the counter. I had watched as his dementia was sliding, little by little. I was grateful we still were able to do some things together. It was a good, warm feeling that took away the frustrations of every day.

30 SOMETHING HAPPENED

My Love had a big smile on his face as our little dog, Mypsy, jumped from the couch and bounded over to see him when he came down the hall toward the living room. Her wagging tail always revealed her happiness that her buddy had come to play.

"We are going to art this morning!" I reminded My Love as he waved at me across the living room.

The cheerfulness on his face disappeared, his shoulders drooped, and his attitude shifted. As usual, any suggestion of something not in his routine, anything he had to be made aware of, created anxiety.

I was trying to develop a habit of not telling him our plans too far in advance. I knew telling him too soon meant anxiety might surface. But I also knew he needed a little wiggle room to get ready before we had to leave. It was my goal to find the right timing, so eventually I could go on auto-pilot. It was my reluctance to deceive My Love that held back my progress.

"Where is that?" he asked. "Where are we going?"

I thought maybe he hadn't heard me.

"Where we always go on Monday morning, to our art class."

I wanted to be clear, I wanted him to be excited, because I knew he loved going to our Monday class. We'd gone for at least four years.

"I never went to an art class."

Well, at least he knows what I said, but something is not right here. Something happened.

"You painted those pictures that are hanging on the wall," I reminded him, as I pointed to the wall we had designated his gallery wall. I hoped he could relate to his own paintings.

"I don't remember making those pictures," he told me as he looked carefully at the framed pictures.

"You always love art class when we go."

Looking around the room, he asked me, "When will I get to go home?"

Did he just shift gears on me? Where did that question came from?

"You are home," I answered.

"This is not home. I want to go to my home."

"Where is your home?" I asked.

He sat down.

"Let me look around here. I don't recognize anything. Nothing is mine," he said as he refocused to see what was in the room he might know.

His remark that "he might know" suggested to me his brain was teetering between reality and a vanishing memory.

"What is happening to me, am I losing my mind?" he asked, rather resigned to the fact that he couldn't identify anything as his own. Still, I felt he trusted the situation because I was there and remained calm.

"Maybe if you sit on the couch for a minute, things might change, and you can see how you feel," I suggested, hoping to give him time to get his bearings, to recognize his surroundings.

I also wanted some time to catch up with what was going on. I should have been ready for his advancing memory loss, but so much had happened in two days that there had been no time to anticipate what would come next. Anyway, who was I kidding? I could not have planned for his memory loss.

Reflecting, it seemed this latest sequence of events had begun on the previous Saturday afternoon when I walked in the door with a small bag of groceries in each hand. I indicated there was one more bag in the car in the parking garage.

"I'll go get it for you," he said, struggling to take the two bags from me.

My Love wanted to help me often. I let him when he could.

"Here, you take the key. The bag is in the back seat." I held out the key for him.

"How do I use this?" he asked, holding the key, looking at the four buttons on the side of my key fob.

I showed him which button to push to lock and unlock. Then I asked him to show me, so I knew he could do it.

"I don't remember right now. But I'll get it," he assured me. Then he added, "Where is the car?"

"In our spot in the basement," I responded.

"Where is that?" he asked in all innocence.

I went to get the last bag.

~

I began to get curious. I wondered if he would forget more in the evenings or if time mattered at all. He had been home alone, waiting about twenty minutes for me as I rushed back from the store. I wondered if his anxiety had elevated his memory loss in some way. *I wish I had paid attention to see if this had happened before!*

I was trying to see if he was developing a specific time of day when elevated memory loss appeared, a time I would know to limit his walking with the dog. I wondered if he reacted the same to a mention of a routine change as well as an actual change. Nothing seemed that simple. I was not a scientist. Would I find answers?

~

I sat straight up, almost as soon as he did. His cough was so loud, his hacking so strong that I woke out of the deepest, soundest sleep I'd had that week. He rarely woke up in the night. Once he fell asleep, he slept through the night. Like a new mother, I felt relief when "my baby" slept, meaning I could too.

But this night the coughing, the hacking, came on suddenly and did not stop. He kept trying to get his breath. It wore me out listening. It wore him out continually trying to clear whatever he sensed was blocking the air passage. Even though he could breathe, he felt like he couldn't. All I could think of was his first COPD exacerbation the previous spring. I didn't want to end up in the hospital again.

For a few moments he would be calm; I hoped we could go back to bed. But then, another strong, noisy burst of air came from his lungs as he hovered over the bathroom sink. And away he went, for a few more minutes, painful hacking and coughing. Even though he was breathing, his need *to feel like* he was breathing was powerful, and the coughing and hacking continued.

When he touched the same place in his chest as he did for all his, dare I say "usual," episodes, I made the connection that this might not be a COPD exacerbation at all, but instead an exaggerated anxiety attack. However, this time it was much stronger. It definitely was louder, and he certainly was fighting harder than he had ever before, just to get a wee spot of phlegm up. I rubbed his back. It did not help. I suggested he stand up straight. He kept coughing. I gave him a glass of water. It made no difference. Only a little phlegm appeared.

I pulled out the little pills and gave him one for under his tongue. He had to hold his mouth closed with his hands, so he wouldn't cough the little pill out. Within thirty minutes he was calm and back in bed. I prayed this was not a new beginning of nightly attacks. I could not survive, and I wondered how he would.

~

A week or two later, as he started to speak, he raised his hand and moved it around the room while pointing to the furniture.

"Who brought all my furniture here, to this place?" he asked.

What did he just ask? What is he talking about?

"What furniture?" I asked him.

"That couch was in our house. That chair, too. And that cabinet against the wall that my dad made. And the rattan coffee table. How did it get here?"

"You and I bought the table and cabinet together years ago," I said. He shook his head no.

"My dad made the table," he said as he stood to touch it. He stripped the wood to make those small pieces on the side." And then he added, "You weren't here then."

He touched the slats of rattan along the edge of the table. My Love was still convinced he had seen his father build the table. Maybe his dad had made something similar once and he was sensing that. Dementia confounded me all the time.

He was convinced his father had built both the cabinet and the coffee table. Had his confusion just started again? At that point I didn't care if My Love believed his father made it all. I did not even understand what changes had just taken place!

"Where are we?" I asked him.

"In this place, I guess." It was obvious he didn't know and did not appear alarmed by not knowing.

After I explained this was our home and the furniture had always been here, I still was not sure My Love trusted my story. But still, something about my having said it seemed to enable him to move on.

~

A day or two later, he was out on the balcony. After he rearranged the chairs for winter, he stood for a moment, holding the railing, and surveyed across the treetops, down the ravine to the river below.

"You know when we were kids, my brother and I used to walk down the stairs to the ground, and down the hill to the river," he said.

As he spoke, he swung around and then looked toward the ground, as if he were watching himself and his brother moving through the yard toward the river. Something similar was in his mind.

"But the river was ice, then," he went on.

He turned to me and showed me with his hands the thickness of the ice. "Ten inches was ice and we walked across the river to that . . ." He had trouble finding the word.". . . building. Only it was a school then."

Whoa! What is going on now?

Confabulations. I had been told they could happen. Or maybe this was a delusion. Maybe a memory distortion, a made-up story to be able to take part in social interaction, common in later stages of dementia. It was not intentional dishonesty. So many tiny differences I didn't know.

"Your family lived here when you were younger?" I asked him.

"Yes, in this apartment, and we walked across that river on the ice," he repeated to me.

There were days I wished I had had a video camera set up that could automatically be switched on without my having to operate it. No one would believe some of the unusual experiences we had been through over the years.

I mentioned the river incident to his twin brother by email. He suggested that perhaps My Love was remembering a time in their teens when their family did live in an apartment for a period. My Love's brother said there was no river, but yes, they had lived in an apartment.

My Love had never told me his family had once lived in an apartment. But it made sense. My Love was confused. Perhaps the memories were melding. Or was he vacillating between reality and his memories?

That same evening, as he made his routine walk to bed, turning out lights and locking the door, he stopped beside me and asked, "When is the lady coming to put me to bed? It is time for bed."

What? What lady? He has never mentioned a lady in his stories of seeing people. I wonder who he means?

"No lady is coming to put you to bed. I put you to bed every night," I told him.

"No. There is another lady who has been coming to give me my medicine and help me get to bed," he insisted.

"Who is the other lady?" I asked.

"I don't know her," was his answer. And then he walked back toward the bedroom, letting the conversation fade away.

Oops . . . another note I better write down for the doctor. I wonder if this is dementia or calcium at work . . . or what?

~

Way too much was going on. It wasn't all dementia nor COPD. It wasn't all his recent pneumonia and not just anxiety. But stirring them all together in the pot created a stressful life for both of us.

His memory loss, at least his vascular dementia, seemed to have dropped another notch. But strangely, he still could tell me about hallucinations he had "seen" earlier in the week, the two men in our hall who called him to go with them, the unknown man and the big dog in our living room, and his brother and someone, but all had come and gone at different times.

He never did mention the lady as part of his sightings. But he was clear as a bell in his recollections nearly a week later as he explained all those he had seen to his doctor. He remembered those short-term memories and actually asked me where those entities had gone!

Dementia boggles my mind. How can anyone study something so erratic?

Every day became an intense learning experience. I seldom planned much. I no longer anticipated anything. I couldn't have expectations of anyone or any activity or relationships. Whatever strange things happened, they remained strange until I had good explanations. I kept going with the flow. I was persevering, patiently staying by My Love while he needed me.

What else could I do?

~

As fall colors faded and the sharp winds blew the leaves to the ground, the chills of winter arrived. During those colder months it was difficult for My Love to get out and walk the dog. He had reduced his path to the space behind our building. But he still walked and then sat on his end of the couch most of the day.

He always had the TV on but was not watching it as much as before. Muting it was fine with him. He played with his phone and his iPad. He still rejected suggestions to paint, even though the paper and paints sat waiting not eight feet away.

Dinner was over, and we had just finished doing the dishes together. I had washed, and he had dried, and I put them away afterward. Standard routine. He was back in his seat and I was at the computer across from him. My desk chair was far better for my aching back than the soft couch, so I sat there even when I wasn't really using the computer.

"Why are you still here?" I heard out of the blue.

"What do you mean?" I answered.

"When are you going to leave? I have some people coming in, people you don't know. I need you to leave before they get here."

I sat in shock. He wasn't joking. I was thinking what my next reaction should be. "I'm not leaving, honey. I live here." I tried to keep a connection between us, but my words meant nothing.

"No, you don't. I'd know if you lived here. Now get out."

"But I take care of you."

"No one takes care of me. I take care of me. Now you get out or I will throw you out."

I didn't know what was going on, but I picked up my cell phone to call his brother.

"Who are you calling?" he asked me.

"Your brother." I was not good at thinking up lies.

"No, put the phone down."

As he spoke, he got up from the couch. I began to realize this was not like his behaviors from before. I had to make the call. But as I lifted the phone to punch in the numbers, he approached me and hit the phone out of my hands.

"You are not calling my brother. You are not calling any one."

He walked into the kitchen. I picked up the cell phone and put it beside my keyboard. Then I started typing an email to his brother to ask guidance. I needed to talk to someone about what was going on.

My Love must have heard the clicking of the keys, because soon he came from the kitchen in a rage, brushed the keyboard to the floor just as I had clicked send. The madman, now inside My Love's body, stood looking at me.

"What do you think you are doing?" he asked. "I told you to leave."

"But I live here, with you," I persisted.

"No, you don't," he repeated. "You have to go!"

Looking back, I should not have argued, but I had never practiced what to do if something strange happened. At first, I did not realize his actions were going to be a threat. I had no idea where the red-line was to call for help. A practice run would have been a great idea. But that could never have happened.

When would have been a good time for that? I didn't have anything to reference before now!

"Can I show you my clothes in the closet? Or pictures of you and me together?" I asked, hoping to find some way he would realize I belonged here, even if he did not know me. Maybe a distraction might work?

"Those aren't your clothes," he said without going to look.

I put my hand on the cell phone and found the call screen, moving only my eyes to look down. I was able to punch in My Love's brother's number.

When I heard him answer I picked up the phone to begin to talk quickly. Within seconds, My Love lunged across the room and grabbed the phone. I had only had time to tell his brother to read the recent email I had sent. Unfortunately, he did not hear me yell for him to call the police before the phone went flying.

My Love began shouting into the phone, "He won't leave. He is staying, and I told him he has to go . . . I am calm . . . But he has to go. I have things to do." He shoved the phone back in my hand.

"I will let you know what happens," I yelled, leaning my head forward over the phone, hoping his brother heard me, because at that instant, My Love again hit the phone to the floor.

Something happened to My Love, and I had no idea what it was. The meds had not changed. The food we had had for dinner was like meals we had eaten many times. His changing brain was in charge and I had no clue what had happened.

"Sit down and let me think about leaving," I said, trying to defuse his anger. I still had trouble grasping it was not My Love I knew saying and doing all this.

"Well, you can sit. But you are leaving," he said as he walked to his seat again.

I sat quiet for only a few minutes.

"Can I give you your meds before I go? There are some that will make you feel better." I hoped I could give him an anxiety pill.

"No. You just want to poison me, to kill me," he said.

Where did that come from?

"That's why I didn't eat my dinner. I know you want to kill me," he went on.

"But your medicine keeps you alive," I said, always realizing after I spoke my words were making no sense to him. He was in his own world.

"Well. How are we going to solve this? You have to go," he said, focused on my leaving.

"I wonder if we have any cookies or chocolate ice cream?" I asked him out of the blue.

"Is there any ice cream?" he asked me. "Do we have some?"

Oh, my gosh! That was almost a complete flip. I couldn't believe what just happened. Another intervention, but of his own doing?

"We can look," I suggested, starting to get up to go look. But he shook his head no and used his hand to tell me to sit back down. I think he forgot the ice cream.

Now what?

Again, I wasn't sure where the words came from, but I heard myself saying, "I can sleep on the couch. I won't disturb your friends."

"And I can sleep in the bed," he answered. "The dog can stay with me."

He had a plan! I wasn't going to argue.

"But it'd be best if you just leave." My Love was back on his rant, just as if he flipped the switch back on.

I got up and walked back to the bedroom. He followed me. I took a framed picture from the wall and handed it to him.

"Who are those two people?" I asked. He looked. Then he saw another with two people. He picked it up to look at it. He looked at the picture, then at me.

"Do you know those two people?" I asked.

"Maybe. That's me. Is that you?"

My counselor had told me earlier that his memory of me might be of my younger self, especially since we had gotten together later in our lives. He might not recognize the living, older me, but pictures of a younger me, he might know. It seemed that might be the case.

"Yes," I said, putting the picture beside my face.

He seemed to be coming out of the wave of anger that had flooded over him. I don't think it was just the pictures that changed him. But he began to settle.

And in a few minutes, he was in bed. I was so relieved, sitting back on the couch, reflecting on what had just happened. Had My Love been in a state of delirium? There was confusion and anxiety. Maybe.

I don't know. I am not a doctor! I can't keep up with all that is going on! His diseases are too overwhelming for me!

And then I saw him coming down the hall. He was coughing with his hand on the center of his chest. I had to get it together for another round!

An episode. He was going to go through an episode. Right then.

"Would you let me give you the little pill for under your tongue now? It might help you get some sleep."

He held out his hand. In under an hour he was back in bed, sleeping. I was a wreck! But alive. I made notes to call the doctor in the morning, to insist on a urine test, to ask what to do. I put the Crisis Emergency Hotline on my phone, with a mental note to advise the agent we were dealing with dementia and Alzheimer's disease, not drugs or alcohol abuse. Evidently, that information assured us that people who were trained for behaviors of dementia would arrive at our home. I could only hope that meant they'd have compassion and heart as well as knowledge and skill.

Good to know!

I knew I was blessed, that the evening before had been my rehearsal for anything similar in the future. I was lucky, I was getting a second chance. I don't think I ever experienced anything worse than feeling there was no escape, feeling I had to stay with him, even in his moments, and maybe hours, of instability. I just couldn't think of those scary movies I had seen, the stories I had read. I had to stay sane.

I would not wait again before calling 911 for help. I would lock myself in the bathroom or go out the door and find help if I had to. I wasn't trained for this and could not wing it again. I would not stay in the unsafe situation thinking I could defuse it by myself. Next time I might not.

Something had happened to My Love. I would be living in that terrorizing space, sitting on pins and needles waiting for the next time. I just didn't know for how long.

~

This event turned out to be somewhat of a significant turning point in My Love's advancing through the course of his diseases. The mixture of all the things that were not right inside him made a confusing life for him, and for me. From this point forward, I was on alert more than ever before. I fine-tuned my focus, reduced my outside thoughts and associations to remain aware of his moment-by-moment changes, and re-directed my activities to be sure I would be safe.

It was best for him to be at home and not out with others. It might have been better for me to be out with others, but that time had to wait. I kept a low profile, remained calm as much as possible, ignored pleas to get out and do things for me. Instead, I remained in a state of caregiving twenty-four seven, so I did not have to switch back and forth with him. More emotions entered our life. More unknowns surfaced. We just kept going, as we all do, no matter what is set before us.

What else could we do?

EPILOGUE

My Love still lives at home at this writing. I believe he knows he is talking to his brother each week when he calls. I do not know what else My Love recalls. We have visited with his brother five or six times a year. My Love's girls, who hold demanding full-time jobs, call and visit when they can. Life goes on. Caregiving does not get easier. I had to tell this story before I couldn't.

Caregivers are a special breed. Strong, sensitive, and compassionate. This was my way to encourage and give hope to caregivers so they could try to **H**ave **O**ne **P**ositive **E**xperience daily, an expression I learned from a local Alzheimer support group.

As our life progressed, of course, dementia did as well. And I aged right along with everyone and everything else! Beyond activities there were personal episodes and emotions that evolved. His disease was full-time; my job was twenty-four seven. I was worn out, yet could not escape.

For My Love, every moment held a flash of potential for a slip in memory, a rise in high calcium, or the appearance of another violent anxiety attack. I lived on pins and needles, wondering every morning as the "Birdsong" played on my phone, what would happen that day.

Caregiving did not stop when the dance was over, or the paints dried up. Our story did not end because the classes and events ceased.

My stresses doubled, my fears never left as new unknowns appeared on a regular basis. And, as always, life went on. As the inevitability of long-term care approached, I had to steel myself for yet one more emotional roller coaster, one inescapable heartache.

Follow us in *Did You Hide the Cookies?* as we share emotions and experiences from day-to-day events, as I continue *Accepting the Gift of Caregiving.*

Accepting the Gift of Caregiving
Support Group

www.CaregiverAlzheimerStory.com

If you, or a caregiver you know, or someone who supports a caregiver, would benefit by having discussions related to dementia or any other caregiving topic, a support group could bring answers, comfort and relief.

Visit website: *www.CaregiverAlzheimerStory.com*

On the website page called 'Discover Support,' the book-related, self-created, support group is explained. My intention is that encouraging a support group could be one more helping hand to those who are still floundering on their caregiving journey.

Find an explanation for the *Accepting the Gift of Caregiving Support Group* and for *Questions for Discovery*, designed for support group discussions.

Remember to keep asking questions.
Judith Allen Shone